AUTHENTIC ASSESSMENT

Authentic Assessment

The Key to Unlocking Student Success

MARK A. BARON, Ph.D.

Assistant Professor, Division of Educational Administration
School of Education, University of South Dakota
Vermillion, South Dakota

FLOYD BOSCHEE, Ed.D.

Associate Professor, Division of Educational Administration
School of Education, University of South Dakota
Vermillion, South Dakota

FOREWORD *by* L. E. SCARR
AFTERWORD *by* ROLAND BARTH

TECHNOMIC
PUBLISHING CO., INC.
LANCASTER · BASEL

Authentic Assessment
a **TECHNOMIC** publication

Published in the Western Hemisphere by
Technomic Publishing Company, Inc.
851 New Holland Avenue, Box 3535
Lancaster, Pennsylvania 17604 U.S.A.

Distributed in the Rest of the World by
Technomic Publishing AG
Missionsstrasse 44
CH-4055 Basel, Switzerland

Printed in the United States of America
10 9 8 7 6 5 4 3 2

Main entry under title:
   Authentic Assessment: The Key to Unlocking Student Success

A Technomic Publishing Company book
Bibliography: p.
Includes index p. 135

Library of Congress Catalog Card No. 95-60887
ISBN No. 1-56676-351-7

Contents

3 ASSESSING INSTRUCTION   41

4 ASSESSING STUDENT PROGRESS   77

5 ASSESSING THE CURRICULUM   91

6 ASSESSING SCHOOL GOVERNANCE AND
EFFECTIVE SCHOOLS   117

Revolution is a word many educators would rather not hear, but it is exactly what is needed if we are to have meaningful ways of assessing student performance. Leading the revolution are Dr. Mark Baron and Dr. Floyd Boschee, with their perceptive observations and research about authentic assessment. Join them, and your students will be better prepared for the future.

The revolutionary battle for educating students' minds could be lost if educators cling to traditional assessment methods. Some children simply are not motivated by a test score or a letter grade based on comparisons with other students. Their potential is locked inside a mind that could excel when given a chance to demonstrate their true knowledge of a subject. In addition, typical appraisals of a student's performance do not give parents or teachers adequate information about the child's abilities.

What is the solution? Authentic assessment—measuring student performance based on tasks that are relevant and useful in real life. These methods include, but are not limited to, student portfolios, oral reports, and reflective journals. Those who believe in authentic assessment are not advocating doing away with all tests of a student's writing ability or computation skills; however, as the authors clearly explain, the key to unlocking student success is in finding superior ways to evaluate one's ability to use diverse academic skills to complete application tasks. In short, are students really learning?

The brilliance of authentic assessment lies in the fact that it is more than a check on how students are doing. It is a tool for instruction . . . a tool that can be used to harvest information about a student's competence.

Clear learning goals, included as a part of the assessment process, make it easier for students to determine what they need to do in order to demonstrate their knowledge. Students soon learn to become active participants in the learning process. Even a young child can begin to see what it takes to achieve success in a certain subject area. As the child grows up, he or she will know how to thrive in school and in life. We must not underestimate the value of that lesson.

If you are committed to improving the quality of learning in your classroom, school building, or school district, I enthusiastically encourage you to read on. The six chapters that follow are a powerful package of information. You will learn new methods for assessing student performance and for assessing curriculum. The authors have also woven threads of knowledge about strategic planning, shared decision making, and developing goals throughout this distinguished tapestry.

If the idea of changing the way you evaluate student performance makes you apprehensive, I urge you to read on. Dr. Baron and Dr. Boschee provide clear and compelling reasons for creating a direct link between student instruction and assessment. Examine their research, study their suggestions, then join the revolution.

L. E. SCARR, ED.D.
Superintendent
Lake Washington School
District
Kirkland, Washington

Great accomplishments have always engendered risk to those who would take the first steps on behalf of those who would follow. Since the earliest days of the Colonial period, Americans have demonstrated a pioneering spirit which has proven instrumental in almost every great accomplishment. From establishment of a democratic form of government through westward expansion and space exploration, American pioneers have always led the way. By accepting the risks involved in charting the unknown, they have empowered the rest of us to safely follow and participate in every great adventure.

During the last decade, this pioneering spirit has pervaded public education in the form of school restructuring and fundamental changes in our view of the educational process. Educational pioneers at every level have accepted the challenge of finding more effective methods to prepare our youth for life in the Twenty-first Century. Each of these methods represents a significant transition from long-held traditional educational beliefs and practices.

Authentic assessment represents one of the most promising innovations being pioneered in school districts throughout the country. Rather than measuring student progress on the basis of seat time or inconsequential test results, authentic assessment proposes measuring student performance on a variety of complex tasks that are meaningful, significant, and useful in real life. Authentic assessment constitutes a system of instructional and assessment practices designed to evaluate a student's ability to use diverse academic skills to complete real-life tasks.

The rapidly changing conditions characterizing our increasingly global society demand that we explore alternative strategies for preparing students to face life after school. Traditional instructional and assessment techniques fail to provide adequate measures of a student's chances for success in a world being transformed by changing social, political, economic, and cultural conditions. Authentic assessment, on the other hand, challenges students to demonstrate proficiency on tasks designed to develop the academic skills essential for successful citizenship in tomorrow's world.

As with all pioneering efforts, the transition to authentic assessment is fraught with difficulties and uncertainty. School districts are wrestling with higher costs and the time requirements associated with a system that utilizes real people rather than machines to develop, deliver, and assess a quality instructional program. Questions have also been raised regarding the reliability and validity of the subjective judgments required by an authentic system of assessment. However, when the educational pioneers have successfully charted a course based on authentic assessment, they will be empowered to prepare all students for their journey through life.

This book examines the process of developing an authentic system of instruction and assessment which will empower educators and students to successfully face the challenges that await them. The process of making the transition to authentic assessment is presented in a systematic, step-by-step fashion.

MARK A. BARON
FLOYD BOSCHEE

We would like to express our sincere appreciation to Marlene J. Lang, instructor and advisor at the Academic Advising and Testing Center, University of South Dakota, Vermillion, for her guidance and editorial advice. We also wish to extend gratitude to our wives, Jackeline Carmen Baron and Marlys Ann Boschee, for their understanding, support, and many valuable suggestions.

We dedicate this book to all the educators who have devoted their professional lives to exploring creative and innovative methods for preparing children for a successful future. These pioneers make it possible for the rest of us to safely participate in the change process that is restructuring American education today.

Chapter 1

INITIATING AUTHENTIC ASSESSMENT

Assessment comprises a process that appraises, evaluates, estimates, or makes a judgment about a performance that can be exhibited, transmitted, executed, shown, or presented in an authentic way, and which constitutes actual, real, or genuine tasks.

Assessment is much more than it used to be. As we enter the Twenty-first Century, we are encountering fundamental changes in the way we view and conduct assessment in American schools. Because sixty years have passed since we experienced such a deep-seated and thoughtful reevaluation of our assessment methods,[1] educators, parents, and interested citizens will likely ask a number of questions about the integral changes to assessment and how they might affect work in classrooms and schools. This book will assist those who are interested in, considering, continuing, and/or advancing authentic assessment procedures. The key questions are as follows:

(*1*) What is authentic assessment?
(*2*) What are the underlying principles of authentic assessment?
(*3*) What needs can authentic assessment fulfill?
(*4*) What are the advantages of authentic assessment?
(*5*) What are the disadvantages of authentic assessment?
(*6*) How does authentic assessment begin?

The answers to these questions, in prescriptive form and outlined in the pages that follow, emerge from theory, research, and observations of practice. Applying reorganized and improved assessment practices will require thoughtful and constant review and attention, and hefty doses of practical wisdom by those who daily confront the infinite variations in all circumstances of assessment.

WHAT IS AUTHENTIC ASSESSMENT?

Authentic assessment is a process where students not only complete or demonstrate desired behaviors, but accomplish them in a real-life context. It "presents tasks that are worthwhile, significant, and meaningful—in short, authentic."[2] Authentic assessment constitutes more than development of better tests; it is dependent on solid classroom teaching practices and various authentic assessment tools to evaluate student learning. The teaching practices and tools should stem from examining questions like "What are we looking for when we assess students' learning? What do we want students to know and understand? What kind of classroom culture nurtures the development of these surroundings? And how can these practices be used to inform teaching and assessment?"[3] Genuine answers to these questions will generate daily classroom teaching practices and student evaluations that drive instruction and learning.

Authentic Assessment and Performance

Authentic assessment "can be defined as any number of methods which may be used to gather information about the performance of students."[4] Authentic assessment encompasses more than student testing and may include gathering information on student performance, student products, and student attitudes or values. Authentic assessment of student performance should be analogous to the real world. For example, when Consumers Union staff assess automobiles to determine rankings within a corresponding group, a performance report with multiple validations is written about each vehicle. Performance reports on one of the "Mid-Priced Sports Sedans"[5] stated that

> ... though the [car's] 2.0-liter Four is the least powerful engine in this group, it provides ample acceleration and averages about 29 mpg on regular fuel. The five-speed manual transmission shifts smoothly, and its gear ratios complement the engine. A four-speed automatic transmission is optional.

The [car] negotiates winding country roads with agility, and the body stays level in wide, sweeping turns. The steering, however, could give more feedback. The car plowed ahead only minimally in hard turns at our test track. It negotiated our avoidance maneuver respectably, with just a bit of tail wag, which our drivers found quite easy to correct.

The [car] needed 136 feet to stop from 60 mph on dry pavement, 149 feet on wet pavement—an average performance. It stopped straight in our tough wet divided-pavement test, where the road is more slippery under the left side of the car than under the right.

We fully understand that cars and students are not alike, but when we assess performance authentically it becomes the same thing. Here the car performed in the real world. The Consumers Union staff assessed several critical performance functions about the cars on a written report for the purpose of giving consumers an accurate picture of mid-sized sports sedan cars. We need to ask: ''Would we have enough information to purchase any one of the mid-priced sports sedans assessed if only the miles-per-gallon performance was reported?'' Likewise with students: ''Do paper-and-pencil tests adequately measure their performance?'' The answer could well be yes *if* we are interested only in memorization and recall of facts.

The strategy for using authentic assessment implies that there will be

- a melange of teaching practices and structures[6]
- multiple validations[7]
- portfolios[8]
- secured tasks[9]

By employing a variety of classroom teaching practices and an assortment of different authentic assessment tools to evaluate student learning, the overall validity of the assessment process becomes enhanced.[10]

WHAT ARE THE UNDERLYING PRINCIPLES OF AUTHENTIC ASSESSMENT?

Essential to authentic assessment is an understanding of the following principles:[11]

(1) The purpose of education is to prepare students to complete life's relevant tasks and to use academic skills in concert to complete those

tasks. Objective type tests (i.e., multiple choice, fill-in-the-blank, matching, or true and false) are *not* helpful indicators for measuring the ability of individuals to complete life's relevant tasks. For example, we want students to learn to love reading and writing, not just to acquire skills in reading and writing. Also, society wants students to practice cooperation, collaboration, citizenship, and democracy, not just read about them. Subsequently, to measure whether students can construct responses rather than simply recall facts from memorized textbooks, authentic assessment approaches prove essential.

(2) *Authentic assessment must be congruent with principles of effective instruction, principles of effective learning and motivation, and principles of effective instructional strategies.* A potentially positive and intended effect of authentic assessment "is that the curriculum and instruction will benefit from a closer match to the test." [12] Well-defined explanations of the principles are presented for each area below.

Principles of Effective Instruction

- *Teacher expectations* means clearly defined learning goals; what it is we want students to know and be able to do.
- *Relevant practice* refers to students completing academically pertinent tasks with a high success rate.
- *Informed feedback* translates to students' understanding of what makes their responses correct or incorrect.
- *Progress evaluation* alludes to assessing students' understanding and using students' performance data to make subsequent instructional decisions.
- *Instructional planning* means to achieve an appropriate instructional match for every student.

Principles of Effective Learning and Motivation

- *Cognitive psychology* connotes that students' performance is enhanced when students are actively engaged (see Figure 1.1

Percentage people generally
remember when they learn by:

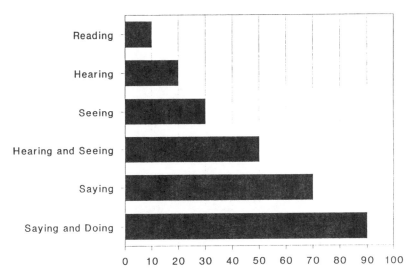

Figure 1.1 Learning to remember.

for data on learning and remembering),[13] considers their prior
knowledge and ties new meaning to existing knowledge,
constructs personal meaning, engages students in self-
monitoring of their progress, encourages students to discuss
their thoughts with others to achieve a deeper level of
meaning, and encourages them to have a clear statement of
expectations.

- *Motivational psychology* implies that students' best work is
most likely to occur when they have choices of and control over
learning, believe assigned tasks have personal relevance,
assume personal responsibility for learning, and have a high
sense of self-efficacy. (For example, using grading criteria for
essays formulates an example of performance-based evaluation
that enhances student motivation. Product-based evaluation,
such as the percentage correct on an objective type test, tends to
decrease motivation, especially for less successful students.)

Principles of Effective Instructional Strategies

- *Cooperative and collaborative learning* strategies have a positive effect on student learning and lend credence to why students need to work together to solve complex, loosely structured problems. (Today's professional and service-oriented work settings require cooperative and collaborative workers.)

The purpose of education should be to create students who have content knowledge as well as the ability to think, solve problems, communicate, and collaborate. For this to happen, teaching methods and "assessment practice must change substantially if [they are] to play a more vital and constructive role in education reform." [14]

WHAT NEEDS CAN AUTHENTIC ASSESSMENT FULFILL?

The criticisms of traditional assessment procedures indicate that they are not complete and our actions based on them are not always wise. The remedy lies in developing better assessment procedures that will give us more complete and more accurate information about the individual. For example, "An A in 11th grade English may mean merely that a student was dutiful and able to fill in blanks on worksheets on juvenile novels. And it remains possible for a student to pass all of his or her courses and still remain functionally and culturally illiterate." [15]

The public is asking: "If kids don't perform, who is responsible and what happens to them?" Since educators are held accountable for students' performance, it is essential that (1) we test what is important to know; (2) we do not rely on tests alone; and (3) we obtain performance data. By using authentic assessment methods we will change tests from after-the-fact devices for checking up on what students have learned to instructional vehicles.

There is little doubt that authentic assessment will engage students in more demanding and realistic tasks and provide teachers with more justifiable instructional targets. We must recognize that authentic assessment

- is designed to be truly representative of performance in the field; only then are the problems of scoring reliability and logistics of testing addressed.

- requires that much greater attention be paid to the teaching and learning of the criteria to be used in the assessment
- promotes self-assessment because it plays a much greater role than in conventional testing
- requires students, in many instances, to present their work and to defend themselves publicly and orally to ensure that their apparent mastery is genuine[16]

A thorough list of authentic assessment attributes follows.

Authentic Assessment Structure and Logistics

- are more appropriately public; involve an audience, a panel, and so on
- do not rely on unrealistic and arbitrary time constraints
- offer known, not secret, questions or tasks
- are more like portfolios or a season of games (not one-shot)
- require some collaboration with others
- recur—and are worth practicing for, rehearsing, and retaking
- make assessment and feedback to students so central that school schedules, structures, and policies are modified to support them

Authentic Assessment Intellectual Design Features

- are "essential"—not needlessly intrusive, arbitrary, or contrived to "shake out" a grade
- are "enabling"—constructed to point the student toward more sophisticated use of the skills or knowledge
- are contextualized, complex intellectual challenges, not "atomized" tasks, corresponding to isolated "outcomes"
- involve the student's own research or use of knowledge, for which "content" is a means
- assess student habits and repertories, not recall or plug-in skills
- are representative challenges—designed to emphasize depth more than breadth
- are engaging and educational
- involve somewhat ambiguous ("ill-structured") tasks or problems

Authentic Assessment Grading and Scoring Standards

- involve criteria that assess essentials, not easily counted (but relatively unimportant) errors
- are not graded on a "curve" but in reference to performance standards (criterion-referenced, not norm-referenced)
- involve demystified criteria of success that appear to students as inherent in successful activity
- make self-assessment a part of the assessment
- use a multifaceted scoring system instead of one aggregate grade
- exhibit harmony with shared schoolwide aims—a standard

Authentic Assessment Fairness and Equity

- ferret out and identify (perhaps hidden) strengths
- strike a constantly examined balance between honoring achievement and native skill or fortunate prior planning
- minimize needless, unfair, and demoralizing comparisons
- allow appropriate room for student learning styles, aptitudes, and interests
- can be—should be—attempted by all students, with the test "scaffolded up," not "dumbed down," as necessary
- reverse typical test-design procedures; they make "accountability" serve student learning (attention is primarily paid to "face" and "ecological" validity of tests)[17]

The attributes of authentic assessment will help to develop a new philosophy of assessment: one that never loses sight of students. "To build such an assessment, we need to return to the roots of authentic assessment, the assessment of performance of exemplary tasks."[18]

WHAT ARE THE ADVANTAGES OF AUTHENTIC ASSESSMENT?

Traditionally, what students assumingly learned could only be assessed through the process of testing, for example, students responding in writing to specific questions which are tangible and structured and administered by teachers within a specific time period. If students did well, average, or poorly on the test, their performance was judged accordingly with a letter grade (A, B, C, D, or F). In essence, one measure was used to assess performance and translated into the amount of learning that transpired. If, however, we examine the concept of authentic assessment closely and honestly, it broadens the view on how students' performance can be measured on the expected outcomes.

Advantages of Authentic Assessment

The advantages of "more authentic" alternative assessment techniques are fourfold:[19]

(*1*) *[Authentic] assessment techniques measure directly what educators want [students] to know.* Because "authentic" testing assumes neither decomposability nor decontextualization, important skills can be tested "holistically" and in context. Holistic and high context testing lead to the mastery of the desired performance.

(*2*) *Authentic assessment techniques emphasize higher thinking skills, personal judgment, and collaboration.* Authentic assessment is designed to create an environment in which students can "show" what they know, leaving the power in their hands and allowing them to utilize higher thinking skills. Performance tests will allow students to write, speak, listen, create, do original research, analyze, and pose and solve problems.

(*3*) *Authentic assessment urges students to become active participants in the learning process.* It helps students to become more involved and responsible for their own learning process. For example, Howard Gardner of Harvard's Project Zero professes that seven basic types of intelligence prevail: linguistic, musical, spatial, logical/mathematical, bodily kinesthetic, interpersonal, and intrapersonal.[20,21] Traditional class time and standardized testing are focused on only two of these types: linguistic and logical/mathematical. Two very important types of intelligence, interpersonal and intrapersonal, are often neglected. On the other hand, most "authentic" testing involves some form of self-criticism and personal evaluation, whether it be editing a piece of writing or critiquing a drawing. It is a well-known fact that well-developed intrapersonal intelligence comprises a common trait in successful individuals. Interpersonal intelligence, the ability to relate with others, is also claimed to be nourished with "authentic" assessment. An example of applying the theory of multiple intelligences occurred when

> Sandy, an elementary student, was struggling with the concept of multiplication. Because she was talented in art, her teacher asked her to create visual representations of the times tables. Sandy dove into the task with relish, drawing configurations of objects to depict "two times two," "two times three," and so on. When she finished, she understood multiplication, because the concept had been expressed through visual images.[22]

By cultivating a broad range of intelligences, teachers can uncover hidden strengths among students who don't shine at verbal or mathematical tasks. Similarly, students who are gifted in a paper-and-pencil environment may be weak in other areas, such as bodily-kinesthetic, spatial, or interpersonal skills.[23]

Many educators today believe that new forms of assessment should be collaborative. They know that in the world beyond school, students will usually have to work and create with others. Rarely does someone in the "real world" create and perform without outside criticism and help.

(4) *Authentic assessment allows and encourages educators to "teach to the test" without destroying validity.* The most important advantage of "authentic" assessment is that it allows tests to be instructional. Rather than be an after-the-fact checkup on students' learning, "authentic" tests can reinforce the curriculum and establish genuine intellectual standards. Consequently, teachers can "teach to the test" without undermining the validity of the test. In fact, with "authentic" assessment, "teaching to the test" is not only possible, it is desirable.[24]

Authentic assessment is a method that is needed in a complex society because we need to discern what students know, what students are able to do, and what students value. Their future is at stake. Contrarily, many still believe that objective type tests (short answer, fifty-six percent, and multiple-choice, fifty-two percent, test questions subsist as the most frequently used by teachers)[25] measure the skills and abilities necessary to perform beyond school. For example, how can short answer or multiple-choice kinds of test questions measure a student's ability to perform on an actual written composition? Such testing can only assume that the student is being taught proper writing skills in the classroom.

WHAT ARE THE DISADVANTAGES OF
AUTHENTIC ASSESSMENT?

There are downsides to authentic assessment that we must recognize.[26] These include the following:

(1) *High cost:* The costs of authentic assessment are automatically substantial because real people, not electronic machines, are required to assess the project or activity. While there are many different estimates of potential cost, clearly authentic assessment requires far more teacher and student time than computer-scored, multiple-choice tests or even than emerging versions of traditional tests adapted to include some open-ended items and other changes. Because few districts or schools have utilized extensive amounts of authentic assessment, actual costs remain undetermined.

(2) *Difficulty in making results consistently quantifiable, objective, standardized, and aggregatable:* The key issue is subjectivity in evaluating performances. It is difficult to assign a specific, adequately discriminating, scaled score or percentile to a more authentic assessment, such as an essay. It is even harder to assign a scaled score or percentile to a portfolio than to have a computer count the number of wrong responses to items on a well-designed objective test.

(3) *Undemonstrated validity, reliability, and comparability of the more subjective scoring systems and their results:* The key issue remains subjectivity in evaluating performances. It is difficult to assign a specific, adequately discriminating scaled score or percentile to a ''more authentic'' assessment, such as an essay, and it is even harder in the case of portfolio evaluations, etc., to have a computer count the number of wrong responses to the items on a well-designed, objective, standardized or teacher made test. Why? Because rarely does a scale on a performance-based assessment contain more than ten points.

Inauspiciously, with authentic assessment it is not possible to answer the question, ''Is this seventh grade doing better or worse than last year's?'' Policymakers want and need to have answers so that they can revise policies, programs, and resources in productive ways. In weighing the advantages and disadvantages of authentic assessment, the authors recommend a mix between alternative, more authentic assessment and traditional standardized measures of academic achievement.

HOW DOES AUTHENTIC ASSESSMENT BEGIN?

Machiavelli[27] said in *The Prince* that "there is nothing more difficult to carry out, nor more doubtful of success, nor more dangerous to handle, than to initiate a new order of things." To prepare for the new order of things, i.e., reformed teaching methods and authentic assessment in a school or district, we must utilize a "systemic reform" process. The process is a strategic planning model[28] that involves all the stakeholders in a community and addresses attitudes, values, and beliefs that underlie education in the community.

To initiate authentic assessment, the classroom structure must change from pedagogical poverty where the teaching acts change from an arrangement of "giving information, asking questions, giving directions, making assignments, monitoring seatwork, reviewing assignments, giving tests, assigning homework, reviewing homework, settling disputes, punishing noncompliance, marking papers, and giving grades,"[29] to exemplary teaching methods that aspire to

- involve students with issues they regard as vital concerns
- engage students with explanations of human differences
- help students to see major concepts, big ideas, and general principles and are not merely engaged in the pursuit of isolated facts
- involve students in planning and what they will be doing
- immerse students with applying ideals such as fairness, equity, or justice to their world
- actively involve students (e.g., participating as a reporter, a role player, or an actor in a small group)
- involve students in real-life experiences
- actively involve students in heterogeneous groups
- ask students to think about an idea in a way that questions common sense or a widely accepted assumption, that relates

new ideas to ones learned previously, or that applies an idea to the problems of living
- absorb students in redoing, polishing, or perfecting their work
- acclimate students with the technology of information access
- empower students to reflect on their own lives and realize how they have come to believe and feel as they do.[30]

To accomplish this, teachers must be given the opportunity to sharpen their pedagogical skills before assessment reform can become reality. The decision to utilize authentic assessment represents a commitment to the idea that all students can learn successfully and that schools create the conditions within which students succeed.

Reorganizing the Carnegie Unit Structure

Educational research and practice suggest that the traditional approach to organizing the high school day (a six- or seven-period day with forty-five- or fifty-minute class periods) may not provide enough time for students to be successful and for teachers to assess authentically. Because "knowledge doesn't come in forty-five- or fifty-minute segments,"[31] several schools around the country have changed from the normal "factory model," six- or seven-period day to a two-, three-, or four-period day for high school students.

The Copernican Plan[32] is one example that is challenging the traditional Carnegie unit structure, which has dominated schools for the last 100 years. For example, seven high schools (six American and one Canadian) serving students from urban, suburban, and rural communities with enrollments ranging from 250 to more than 1,500 students used six different versions of the Copernican schedule. A comparison of the Copernican-schedule high schools versus Carnegie-schedule high schools after one year revealed that the Copernican-schedule schools

- had favorable pedagogical outcomes
- impacted student attendance positively
- showed reductions in the rate of student suspension, ranging from twenty-five percent to seventy-five percent
- reduced student dropout rates
- increased academic mastery ranging from zero percent to forty-six percent. The median increase for all Copernican-schedule schools was eighteen percent.

Research by W. Edwards Deming disclosed that "85% of an organization's problems are usually caused by the system; only about 15% are related to poor performance of staff." [33] As we consider systemic change, "there is no professional reason for delay; in fact, continuing with the present traditional Carnegie structure raises the serious question of professional malpractice." [34]

REVIEW ACTIVITIES

(*1*) What forms/types of assessment are utilized in your school or district? How much assessment consists of multiple-choice, true-false, matching, and fill-in-the blank tests? How much consists of question and answer activities?

(*2*) Discuss advantages of authentic assessments.

(*3*) Discuss disadvantages of authentic assessments.

(*4*) Brainstorm alternative authentic assessments to replace the "traditional" assessments as listed in Review Activity #1.

(*5*) Envision how the school day/class period and assessment strategies could be changed in your school system.

ENDNOTES

1 Stiggins, R. J. 1991. "Facing the Challenges of a New Era of Educational Assessment," *Applied Measurement in Education,* 4:263.

2 Archbald, D. A. and F. M. Newmann. 1988. *Beyond Standardized Testing: Assessing Authentic Achievement in The Secondary Schools.* Reston, VA: National Association of Secondary School Principals, p. 1.

3 Zessoules, R. and H. Gardner. 1991. "Authentic Assessment: Beyond the Buzzword and Into the Classroom," in *Expanding Student Assessment,* V. Perrone, ed., Alexandria, VA: Association for Supervision and Curriculum Development, p. 70.

4 Kulieke, M. J. 1991. "Assessing Outcomes of Significance," *Outcomes,* 9(4):25.

5 Consumers Union. 1994. "Mid-Priced Sports Sedans," *Consumer Reports,* (November):738.

6 Boschee, F. and M. A. Baron present teaching strategies such as production-driven learning, problem-based learning, authentic research and learning, off-the-page learning, reenactment learning, and technology and learning, as well as classroom structures such as small groups, brainstorming, and heterogeneous grouping as examples to enhance authentic learning in *Outcome-Based Education: Developing Programs Through Strategic Planning.* 1993. Technomic Publishing Company, Inc., pp. 80–89.

7 Chapter 3 provides an explanation of multiple validations. For additional informa-

tion see Boschee, F. and M. A. Baron. 1993. *Outcome-Based Education: Developing Programs Through Strategic Planning.* Lancaster, PA: Technomic Publishing Company, Inc., pp. 105 – 113.

8 A detailed explanation of portfolios is presented in Chapter 3. For additional information see Boschee, F. and M. A. Baron. 1993. *Outcome-Based Education: Developing Programs Through Strategic Planning.* Lancaster, PA: Technomic Publishing Company, Inc., pp. 113 – 115.

9 Chapter 3 presents a detailed explanation of secured tasks. For additional information see Boschee, F. and M. A. Baron. 1993. *Outcome-Based Education: Developing Programs Through Strategic Planning.* Lancaster, PA: Technomic Publishing Company, Inc., pp. 115 – 116.

10 Boschee, F. and M. A. Baron. 1993. *Outcome-Based Education: Developing Programs Through Strategic Planning.* Lancaster, PA: Technomic Publishing Company, Inc., p. 105.

11 Christensen, S. L. 1991. "Authentic Assessment: Straw Man or Prescription for Progress?" *School Psychology Quarterly,* 6:294 – 297.

12 Miller, M. D. and S. M. Legg. 1993. "Alternative Assessment in a High-Stakes Environment," *Educational Measurement: Issues and Practice,* 12(2):9.

13 Adapted from Alcorn, M. D., J. S. Kinder, and J. R. Schunert. 1970. *Better Teaching in Secondary Schools.* Chicago, IL: Holt, Rinehart and Winston, Inc., p. 216.

14 Archbald, D. A. 1991. "Authentic Assessment: Principles, Practices, and Issues," *School Psychology Quarterly,* 6:281.

15 Wiggins, G. 1989. "A True Test: Toward More Authentic and Equitable Assessment," *Phi Delta Kappan,* 70(9):704.

16 ———. 1989. "Teaching to the (Authentic) Test," *Educational Leadership,* 46(7):45.

17 ———. 1989. "Teaching to the (Authentic) Test," *Educational Leadership,* 46(7):45.

18 ———. 1989. "A True Test: Toward More Authentic and Equitable Assessment," *Phi Delta Kappan,* 70(9):712.

19 Hacker, J. and W. Hathaway. 1991. "Toward Extended Assessment: The Big Picture," paper presented at the *Annual Conference of the American Educational Research Association,* Chicago, IL.

20 Gardner, H. and T. Hatch. 1989. "Multiple Intelligences Go to School: Educational Implications of the Theory of Multiple Intelligences," *Educational Researcher,* 18(8):6.

21 According to Howard Gardner's theory of multiple intelligences, all people possess seven distinct sets of capabilities. These intelligences work in concert, not in isolation. The seven intelligences, adapted from the ASCD book *Multiple Intelligences in the Classroom* by Thomas Armstrong, are:

- *Spatial:* The ability to perceive the visual-spatial world accurately and to perform transformations upon one's perceptions. This intelligence is highly developed in hunters, scouts, guides, interior designers, architects, artists, and inventors.
- *Bodily-Kinesthetic:* Expertise in using one's whole body to express ideas and feelings and facility in using one's hands to produce or transform things. Highly developed in actors, mimes, athletes, dancers, craftspersons, sculptors, mechanics, and surgeons.
- *Musical:* The capacity to perceive, discriminate, transform, and express musical forms. Highly developed in musical performers, aficionados, and critics.

- *Linguistic:* The capacity to use words effectively, either orally or in writing. Highly developed in storytellers, orators, poets, playwrights, editors, and journalists.
- *Logical-Mathematical:* The capacity to use numbers effectively and to reason well. Highly developed in mathematicians, tax accountants, statisticians, scientists, computer programmers, logicians.
- *Interpersonal:* The ability to perceive and make distinctions in the moods, intentions, motivations, and feelings of other people. This intelligence can include sensitivity to facial expressions, voice, gestures, as well as the ability to respond effectively to such cues – for example, to influence other people.
- *Intrapersonal:* Self-knowledge and the ability to act adaptively on the basis of that knowledge. This intelligence includes having an accurate picture of one's strengths and limitations, awareness of one's moods and motivations, and the capacity for self-discipline.

22 Association for Supervision and Curriculum Development. 1994. "The Well-Rounded Classroom: Applying the Theory of Multiple Intelligences," *Update.* Alexandria, VA: Association for Supervision and Curriculum Development, 36(8):1.

23 ———. 1994. "The Well-Rounded Classroom: Applying the Theory of Multiple Intelligences," *Update.* Alexandria, VA: Association for Supervision and Curriculum Development, 36(8):1.

24 Resnick, C. B. 1989. "Tests as Standards of Achievement in Schools," paper prepared for the *Educational Testing Service Conference: The Uses of Standardized Tests in American Education,* New York.

25 Fray, R. B., L. H. Cross, and L. J. Weber. 1993. "Testing and Grading Practices and Opinions of Secondary Teachers of Academic Subjects: Implications for Instruction in Measurement," *Educational Measurement: Issues and Practice,* 12(3):25.

26 Hacker, J. and W. Hathaway. 1991. "Toward Extended Assessment: The Big Picture," paper presented at the *Annual Conference of the American Educational Research Association,* Chicago, IL.

27 Machiavelli, N. 1965. *The Prince.* New York: Airmont (Original work published in 1513).

28 For a strategic planning model, see Boschee, F. and M. A. Baron. 1993. *Outcome-Based Education: Developing Programs Through Strategic Planning.* Lancaster, Pa: Technomic Publishing Company, Inc., pp. 27–48.

29 Haberman, H. 1991. "The Pedagogy of Poverty Versus Good Teaching," *Phi Delta Kappan,* 73:291.

30 ———. 1991. "The Pedagogy of Poverty Versus Good Teaching," *Phi Delta Kappan,* 73:293–294.

31 Valdez, G. July 22, 1992. "Champlin Park In A Class By Itself." R. Hotakainen (Staff Writer), *Star Tribune,* Minneapolis, MN: p. 8A.

32 For a description of the Copernican plan, see Carroll, J. M. 1989. *The Copernican Plan: Restructuring the American High School.* Andover, MA: Regional Laboratory for Educational Improvement of the Northeast and Islands.

33 Carroll, J. M. 1994. "The Copernican Plan Evaluated: The Evolution of a Revolution," *Phi Delta Kappan,* 76:108–113.

34 ———. 1994. "The Copernican Plan Evaluated: The Evolution of a Revolution," *Phi Delta Kappan,* 76:113.

Chapter 2

PLANNING FOR ASSESSMENT

No one plans to fail, they only fail to plan.

The expression, "If you don't know where you're going, you won't know when you get there," holds special relevance for those engaged in creating a strategy for assessing students' long-term progress. Identifying significant learner outcomes that provide an adequate basis and framework for reliable assessment requires careful planning by educators, parents, students, and members of the school's community (all of the school's stakeholders).

STRATEGIC PLANNING

Strategic planning provides the roadmap that charts the direction students will take throughout their educational journey. The strategic planning process produces a map that not only displays a variety of routes leading to the final destination (learner exit outcomes), but also furnishes recognizable landmarks that indicate how much progress has been made toward reaching that destination.

Within an educational setting, strategic planning provides a process for identifying desired learner outcomes based upon shared visions of an ideal future. Unlike traditional long-range planning that produces blueprints for making future decisions, strategic planning articulates a vision of the future to guide current decision making.[1] It enables all educational stakeholders to collectively identify and create a preferred

17

future for the school district or an individual school. In essence, strategic planning represents "long-term planning with a vision." [2]

Strategic planning constitutes a proactive, future-oriented approach that enables stakeholders to take the initiative in creating learning environments that encourage and support authentic assessment. The planning process culminates in a set of learner exit outcomes that define the knowledge, skills, and attitudes that will enable all students to succeed in life. These learner exit outcomes provide the framework for transforming current instructional and assessment practices into a system of authentic assessment where significant learning is demonstrated in a real-life context. Through the strategic planning process, educational stakeholders should develop a district philosophy, a district vision, a district mission, and a set of learner exit outcomes.

ESTABLISHING PLANNING TEAMS

Shared decision making is the cornerstone of the strategic planning process. Collaborative planning and problem solving improve the quality of decisions and increase stakeholders' satisfaction with the planning process and its results.

Planning team members should be "well-informed, articulate people of good will who represent particular perspectives on the school district." [3] They should possess sufficiently well-developed human relations skills to interact effectively with other members of the planning team and community. Most importantly, planning team members must be committed to a change process that will restructure instruction and assessment within every school throughout the district. Among the district stakeholder groups represented on the planning team should be:

- the board of education
- central office administration
- building-level administration
- teachers (from all instructional levels)
- noncertified district personnel
- local university and/or educational extension personnel
- parents (PTA and other parent groups)
- community groups (business/civic/religious)
- students

In addition to the district planning team, each school building within the district should form a planning team to translate the district's strategic plan into a site-based plan. Each site planning team will determine how to take maximum advantage of locally available resources to achieve the district's mission in their own buildings. Site-based implementation of the district's plan enhances local ownership of the plan and increases local accountability for student performance and success. One assistant superintendent in a school district successfully implementing strategic planning noted that

> Schools are the playing fields for the actions of the district. . . . Site-based planning in the context of strategic planning gives the school and the district the opportunity to work together in harmony to ensure success for every child in the 21st century.[4]

Members of the site planning team for each school building should include:

- the principal and/or assistant principal(s)
- teachers from each grade level/content (subject) area
- noncertified building personnel
- parents
- local community/neighborhood groups
- students

Whenever possible, at least one member of the site planning team should also serve as a member of the district planning team to act as a liaison between the two groups.

BUILDING SUPPORT FOR STRATEGIC PLANNING

Successful educational reform through strategic planning requires substantial understanding of the planning process and genuine commitment from all stakeholders to see it through. Therefore, mounting an effective public relations campaign through "regular communications with *all* parties at *all* phases of the process"[5] is crucial. Once the district has decided to engage in strategic planning, educators, parents, and community members must be apprised of how the process works, how specific groups and individuals will be involved, how long each step in the process will take, and what results and potential benefits can be expected. As the planning process proceeds, community stakeholders must continually be informed of progress being made and must be given the opportunity to provide both positive and negative feedback. The following outlines some of the activities that promote an effective public relations campaign.

(*1*) Provide comprehensive training for site-based planners, including strategies for public relations with district stakeholders, for all district planning team members.

(*2*) District planning team members should provide training, explain the strategic planning process, describe plans for implementation, and provide hand-out materials to all site planning team members who, in turn, share this information with teachers and noncertified personnel in each of their buildings.

(*3*) District planning team members should then sponsor a series of town meetings with as many different community focus groups as possible to explain the strategic planning process, answer questions, gather feedback, and solicit support.

(*4*) Site planning team members from each school building should conduct a series of neighborhood meetings (possibly held in the school building) with as many different local focus groups and parents as possible to describe specific site-based activities, discuss possible focus group participation, and stimulate discussion.

(*5*) As the strategic planning process and implementation proceed, district and site planning team members should regularly apprise individuals and groups throughout the district of their progress while continually soliciting feedback. Sharing of information with educators and community members could take place through
- regularly scheduled face-to-face meetings at school buildings and various locations in the community
- regularly published bulletins or newsletters
- informational announcements in local newspapers or on local radio and television broadcasts
- interactive electronic media such as electronic bulletin boards or other commercial on-line computer services

PLANNING TO PLAN

Having established support for strategic planning throughout the community, the district planning team must begin to outline the activities that will comprise the actual planning process. Prior to developing the strategic plan, decisions must be made regarding what needs to be produced, who needs to be involved, what resources will be required, and when these products need to be completed. This planning-to-plan process results in an action plan that provides direction for formulating the district philosophy, vision, mission, and learner exit outcomes. The process also furnishes planning team members with more detailed information that can be shared with community stakeholders to increase understanding and continue building support for strategic planning.

The following briefly summarizes the steps involved in planning-to-plan:[6]

(*1*) The district planning team is divided into work groups of four to eight members who represent diverse interests within the school system and community. One member is selected to serve as a facilitator for the group.

(*2*) Each work group determines what needs to be decided, who should be responsible, and completion dates for the formulation of a district philosophy, vision, mission, and set of learner exit outcomes.

(*3*) One or two members of each work group meet with each other in a consensus group to review each work group's ideas and incorporate them into a plan to create a district philosophy. Other consensus groups follow the same procedures to create the district vision, mission, and set of learner exit outcomes.

(*4*) Members of each consensus group return to their original work groups to share plans formulated by the consensus groups and either accept the plans or suggest changes.

(*5*) Consensus groups reconvene to continue modifying plans until they are acceptable to all members of the planning team.

IDENTIFYING SIGNIFICANT FUTURE TRENDS

One important underlying principle of authentic assessment asserts that the purpose of education is to prepare individuals to complete life-relevant tasks and to use academic skills in concert to complete a task.[7] Due to rapidly changing social, cultural, political, economic, and environmental conditions, the world in which today's students will live and work will be significantly different from the present. Therefore, everyone involved in the strategic planning process must be aware of future global trends and conditions that will determine what knowledge, skills, and attitudes will be relevant for today's students in tomorrow's world.

District and site planning teams should conclude the planning-to-plan phase of their strategic planning process by closely examining significant future trends and their implications for transforming current instructional and assessment practices. Activities designed to inform planning team members might include the following:[8]

(1) Collect information from a variety of sources regarding major changes taking place in the United States and throughout the world. Several books that critically examine future trends and their consequences include:
- *Future Edge* by Joel Barker[9]
- *Workplace 2000* by Joseph Boyett and Henry Conn[10]
- *Trend Tracking* by Gerald Celente and Tom Milton[11]
- *Schools of the Future* by Marvin Cetron[12]
- *Global Paradox* by John Naisbitt[13]
- *Megatrends 2000* by John Naisbitt and Patricia Aburdene[14]
- *Schools for the 21st Century* by Phillip Schlechty[15]
- *Powershift* by Alvin Toffler[16]

(2) Identify and prioritize future trends and conditions from all of the collected materials that appear most relevant and significant.[17]

(3) Select five to ten of the future trends considered most significant by the largest proportion of planning team members (and other stakeholders) involved in the activity.

(4) Examine the five to ten most significant future trends and discuss the probable impact they will have on society, and the specific knowledge, skills, and attitudes that students will require to succeed in a society impacted by these trends.

DEVELOPING THE STRATEGIC PLAN

Having established the planning framework through the planning-to-plan process and considering significant future trends and their implications, the district planning team now proceeds to develop the strategic plan. This process involves creating a district philosophy, vision, mission, and set of learner exit outcomes.[18]

Developing the District Philosophy

The district philosophy reflects stakeholders' collective beliefs regarding the roles and responsibilities of students, school staff, parents, and community members in the district's educational process. Beliefs define the local educational culture by characterizing *how things get done* (or *how things* should *get done*) in the school or district.

Since the district philosophy provides the framework for strategic planning and identifying desired learner outcomes, beliefs comprising the philosophy must be consistent with principles and practices that promote authentic assessment. Although every belief comprising the district philosophy need not directly address authentic assessment, planning team members should avoid incorporating any beliefs that would greatly obstruct the authentic assessment process. Figure 2.1 presents a brief example of a school district philosophy.[19]

The process for identifying district planning team members' beliefs is similar to the process previously described for reaching consensus during the planning-to-plan phase. The following basic steps summarize this process.

(*1*) Divide the district planning team into work groups of four to eight members with one member chosen as a facilitator.

(*2*) Have each work group generate a list of beliefs regarding students, school staff, parents, and community members.

(*3*) Direct one or two members of each work group to meet with each other in a consensus group to formulate a prioritized list of belief statements regarding students. Other consensus groups should follow the same procedures to develop a set of belief statements for school staff, parents, and community members.

(*4*) Members of each consensus group should return to their original work groups to share belief statements formulated by the consensus groups and either accept the plans or suggest changes.

(*5*) Consensus groups should then reconvene to continue revising belief statements, integrate similar statements, and prioritize statements regarding each target group until they are acceptable to all members of the planning team.

(*6*) After the district planning team selects the five to ten beliefs regarding students, school staff, parents, and community members that will comprise the district philosophy, a final copy of the district

The Learner

- Learning is a continuous process during which each person needs to develop:
  - communication, problem solving, decision making skills, and computational skills.
  - independent learning and group participation skills for self-directed learning.
- Each person needs to become an increasingly effective citizen of the home, school, community, nation, and world.

The School Staff

- Each school staff member influences the way in which the individual learner experiences the curriculum, uses instructional time, materials, and assessment measures, and is evaluated.
- The probability of learning increases when each school staff member uses varied learning plans that provide for:
  - the unique learning styles of individual learners.
  - the individual's rate of learning.
  - active individual participation in learning.

The Parent

- The parent should have a variety of opportunities to be involved in the school.
- The parent has the responsibility to be informed about and involved in decisions that affect education throughout the community.

The Community

- The community has the responsibility to provide for the learning needs of all.
- The community should work with the schools and all other public and private, formal and informal community agencies to provide for the growth needs of citizens of all ages.

Figure 2.1 Example of a district philosophy.

philosophy should be distributed to each member of the planning team and shared with stakeholder groups throughout the community.

Conducting a Beliefs Analysis

A beliefs analysis compares current educational practices in the school or district to stakeholders' expressed beliefs regarding exemplary practices. In essence, the analysis identifies discrepancies between *what is* happening and *what should be* happening in classrooms and schools throughout the district. Discrepancies identified through the beliefs analysis serve as a focus for making important decisions regarding desired learner exit outcomes and methods for achieving those outcomes. The following illustrates an example of a beliefs analysis for one of the belief statements previously presented:

(*1*) *Belief:* Learning at all ages is a continuous process during which each person needs to develop independent learning and group participation skills for self-directed learning.

(*2*) *What Happens:* To maintain classroom order and discipline, students work independently almost all of the time and have little opportunity to work in group settings.

(*3*) *What Should Happen:* Teachers must create learning situations that provide an adequate opportunity for each student to work in group settings, as well as individually, to solve problems.

When combined, *what should happen* statements regarding students, school staff, parents, and community members portray an ideal vision of educational practice consistent with stakeholder beliefs and principles of authentic assessment.

The following briefly summarizes the steps involved in conducting a beliefs analysis.

(*1*) Divide the district planning team into four groups of approximately equal size. Each group will address belief statements regarding one target group (students, school staff, parents, and community members).

(*2*) For each belief statement, members of each group collectively write one *what happens* statement and one *what should happen* statement.

(*3*) When completed, members of each group share their statements with the planning team as a whole who discuss each set of statements until consensus is reached regarding all statements for each target group.

Developing the District Vision

The district vision portrays an image of what the educational process in the district will (or should) look like in the future. Based upon identified beliefs, significant future trends, and results of the beliefs analysis, the vision represents a shared view of the preferred educational future for the district. A clearly articulated vision motivates planners to move in a common direction and provides a yardstick by which to measure progress toward the preferred future. The following presents a sample vision statement emerging from previously presented belief statements for each target group.

Within five years, the Hometown Public School system will be a place where:

- Students acquire and demonstrate group participation and problem-solving skills through continual active involvement in group-oriented authentic tasks.
- School staff provide the maximum opportunity for the individual growth of every student by utilizing authentic tasks and other pedagogical methods that provide for the unique learning styles of every individual student.
- Parents are provided with ample opportunity to spend quality instructional time in the classroom through participation in the learning activities of the children.
- Educational opportunities provided by community members outside of the classroom assist students in applying what they learn in school to real-life problems and situations.

Each statement comprising the district vision depicts what would happen following implementation of each of the *what should happen* statements from the beliefs analysis.

Development of a district vision may be accomplished in the following manner.

(*1*) The district planning team is divided into four groups of approximately equal size—one group each for students, school staff, parents, and community members.

(2) Each group writes one vision statement to correspond with each of the *what should happen* statements resulting from the previous beliefs analysis.

(3) When completed, members of each group share their vision statements with the planning team as a whole who discuss each set of statements until a consensus is reached regarding all statements for each target group. A final copy of the district vision is distributed to each member of the planning team and shared with stakeholder groups throughout the community.

Developing the District Mission

The district mission represents the overall educational purpose of the school district. Stated in broad terms, the mission creates meaning and provides general direction for district educators and stakeholders. It must correspond to the district's philosophy and vision, be stated in future-oriented terms to address student's future needs, and be general enough to encompass all learner exit outcomes. The following represent several mission statements already adopted by school districts.

- empowering all students to succeed in a changing world[20]
- to develop lifelong learners who value themselves, contribute to their community, and succeed in a changing world[21]
- lifelong learning for all[22]

The following steps provide a brief outline of the process for developing a district mission.

(1) The planning team is divided into brainstorming groups of approximately four to eight members.

(2) Members of each group carefully examine significant future trends, the district philosophy, beliefs analysis, and district vision previously developed by the planning team.

(3) Members of each group propose mission statements based on their examination of previously developed documents and the group discusses and revises these statements until they can reach consensus on a single statement.

(*4*) Each group shares its proposed mission statement with the entire planning team, who compare and revise these statements until they develop a single statement which is satisfactory to all members of the team. A final copy of the district mission is distributed to each member of the planning team and shared with stakeholder groups throughout the community.

Developing Learner Exit Outcomes

The culminating step in the strategic planning process consists of articulating a set of learner exit outcomes and associated proficiencies that describe the knowledge, skills, and attitudes that all students will be expected to demonstrate by the time they graduate. Learner exit outcomes, which relate to real-world knowledge and skills, establish the criteria by which successful teaching and learning will be evaluated. When integrated with program (content area) goals, learner exit outcomes and proficiencies ''are the components around which performance assessment, curriculum, and instruction are organized.''[23] Effective learner exit outcomes:

- consist of five to eight broad statements that describe the knowledge, skills, and attitudes needed by all students to succeed following graduation from school
- include a list of measurable proficiencies that indicate the degree to which each outcome has been achieved
- focus on real-world roles and responsibilities
- provide sufficient direction to drive curriculum development and assessment practices
- relate to ends rather than means

Figure 2.2 illustrates an example of learner exit outcomes and accompanying proficiencies.[24]

Identifying learner exit outcomes consists of two related activities, developing the broad exit outcomes themselves and identifying a set of proficiencies or performance indicators for each exit outcome. The following procedure outlines the process for developing learner exit outcomes.

(*1*) The planning team is divided into work groups of about four to eight members; a facilitator is selected for each group.

Self-Directed Learner

- sets priorities and achievable goals
- monitors and evaluates progress
- creates options for self
- assumes responsibility for actions
- creates a positive vision for self and future

Collaborative Worker

- monitors own behavior as a group member
- assesses and manages group functioning
- demonstrates interactive communication
- demonstrates consideration for individual differences

Complex Thinker

- uses a wide variety of strategies for managing complex issues
- selects strategies appropriate to the resolution of complex issues and applies the strategies with accuracy and thoroughness
- accesses and uses topic-relevant knowledge

Quality Producer

- creates products that achieve their purpose
- creates products appropriate to the intended audience
- creates products that reflect craftsmanship
- uses appropriate resources/technology

Community Contributor

- demonstrates knowledge about his or her diverse communities
- takes action
- reflects on role as a community contributor

Figure 2.2 Example of learner exit outcomes.

(2) Each group selects one significant future trend previously identified and examines all future conditions likely to result from that trend. They incorporate any other significant future trend(s) that might impact upon the selected trend. (For example, *increasingly rapid worldwide communication* and *increasing rate of knowledge acquisition and dissemination* would both result in a society where successful citizens will be required to access and transmit information quickly and effectively.)

(3) Each group proposes one general learner exit outcome that describes an individual who is able to function effectively within the identified future condition associated with their trend.

(4) Prior to final acceptance, each group examines and, if necessary, modifies its proposed exit outcome to assure that it is consistent with the district philosophy, vision, and mission.

(5) Each group lists all possible proficiencies that would indicate that a student had achieved the exit outcome that was developed. Group members examine the list, and integrate or combine similar proficiencies until consensus is reached regarding the list of proficiencies.

(6) When completed, members of each group share their learner exit outcomes with the planning team as a whole, who discuss each set of statements until consensus is reached for all exit outcomes and proficiencies. A final copy of the district exit outcomes and accompanying proficiencies is distributed to each member of the planning team and shared with stakeholder groups throughout the community.

INCORPORATING LEARNER EXIT OUTCOMES INTO PROGRAM DEVELOPMENT

Since learner exit outcomes and proficiencies focus on demonstrating real-world knowledge, skills, and attitudes, they inherently lend themselves to an instructional system based on authentic assessment. However, successful achievement of these learner exit outcomes and proficiencies requires incorporating relevant knowledge, skills, and attitudes into several successively more specific levels of content-related instruction and assessment.

Although community stakeholders as well as educators have a major role in identifying learner exit outcomes and associated proficiencies, educators should assume the primary responsibility for integrating these proficiencies into the instructional program. The school administrators, teachers, and educational specialists comprising program (content or subject area) committees must utilize relevant training and experience to design pedagogically sound programs that promote principles of authentic assessment, and that embrace the district's philosophy, vision, and mission.

Program Committees

Program committees are comprised of relevant content area teachers representing all the grade levels (K – 12) operating throughout the school district. (For example, a social science program committee would consist of at least one teacher from each elementary grade level and one social science teacher from each middle/junior high and high school grade level.) Each committee should also contain at least one building principal, assistant principal, or designee. Whenever possible, the school district curriculum director (or designee) should serve as chair of each committee. Program committee members will develop a program philosophy and identify program outcomes and appropriate instructional outcomes for each instructional level and unit within their respective content area.[25]

Program Philosophy

A program philosophy describes the overall purpose or rationale for including the program in the curriculum. The philosophy provides direction for development of program outcomes (goals) and assures that the program will incorporate important elements of the district's philosophy, vision, mission, and learner exit outcomes. The following illustrates an example of a social science program philosophy.[26]

In order to function productively in a changing world, students must develop an understanding of themselves and society. The skills and knowledge obtained through the social sciences will help young people meet the challenges of a dynamic and increasingly complex world. Specifically, social sciences will assist students to develop

- a perspective of cultures and multiethnic societies that respects the dignity and worth of all people
- an ability to participate in a democratic society
- an ability to acquire information and ideas from a variety of sources, time periods, and perspectives to use to analyze and resolve complex issues
- connections between people and their heritage, values, environments, and economic and political systems
- an ability to use all of the social sciences as tools to investigate and solve real-life problems

Program Outcomes

Program outcomes (or goals) provide evidence of the learning that takes place in each discipline or instructional program (content area) from kindergarten through twelfth grade. Guided by the program philosophy, program outcomes incorporate learner exit outcome proficiencies into the curriculum for each instructional program area, providing the context in which students will acquire and demonstrate real-world knowledge, skills, and attitudes. Successful achievement of program outcomes for all content areas provides evidence of subject matter proficiency in each area and effective use of exit outcome proficiencies within the context of each content area. The following provides an example of program outcomes for the social sciences.[27]

Each student will:

- analyze how people are affected by and adapt to different physical and cultural environments
- analyze democratic and constitutional principles and practices and demonstrate the ability to take action within the political system
- examine local, national, and international issues and conflicts from a variety of perspectives and determine how they impact life today
- demonstrate the ability to evaluate and analyze historical evidence to formulate viewpoints and plan for the future
- identify the goals, performance, and problems of economic and political systems and analyze how nations are interdependent

- analyze how individuals and groups respond to social conditions and pressures

Achievement of these program outcomes provides evidence that students have mastered the major concepts of the social sciences through application of the knowledge, skills, and attitudes described by the district's learner exit outcome proficiencies.

The following briefly summarizes the process of developing program outcomes:

(*1*) Using the program philosophy as a framework, members of the program committee (or a selected subcommittee) gather information regarding content area standards from a variety of available sources. Potential sources for standards and information include

- national curriculum groups (such as the National Councils of Teachers of Mathematics, Social Studies, Science, and English)
- state curriculum frameworks
- groups engaged in school restructuring efforts (such as Coalition of Essential Schools)
- frameworks developed for national and international assessments (such as the National Assessment of Educational Progress – NAEP)[28]

(*2*) Committee members examine and interpret the gathered information to identify several prominent themes or content domains that will be emphasized throughout the K – 12 curriculum.

(*3*) One program outcome is developed for each of the identified themes or content domains. Generally, a total of five to ten program outcomes will encompass the majority of content area concepts and provide sufficient direction for the subsequent development of more specific learner outcomes.

Learner Outcomes

Learner outcomes represent clearly defined demonstrations of learning related to particular knowledge, skills, or attitudes within a specific content area for an appropriate developmental level. Accomplishment of a learner outcome could represent the culmination of one instructional unit; however, very long or complex units might require students to demonstrate several related learner outcomes for completion. It is also conceivable that accomplishment of one learner outcome might represent the completion of several instructional units or parts of several units.

Cumulative accomplishment of learner outcomes must facilitate achievement of previously identified program outcomes. Over the course of the $K-12$ program of studies, successful completion of all assigned learner outcomes must ensure that the student has met all program outcomes identified for each content area. Additionally, grade-level promotion and course completion will be contingent upon successful completion of all assigned learner outcomes comprising the grade level or course. (Chapter 4 presents detailed information regarding assessment of learner outcomes for grade-level promotion and course completion.)

The following list outlines the steps involved in developing appropriate learner outcomes.

(*1*) Members of each program committee form subgroups based on the grade levels and content areas taught (for example, primary, elementary, middle level, and high school subgroups).

(*2*) Members of each subgroup reexamine information regarding curricular standards gathered during the development of program outcomes. Particular attention is given to information and standards related to appropriate instructional outcomes for specific grade levels and courses.

(*3*) One or more learner outcomes is identified for each grade level or course which corresponds to at least one program outcome.

(*4*) Learner outcomes are arranged in proper sequence within each grade level or course.

(*5*) The program committee as a whole reconvenes to review and analyze learner outcomes for all grade levels and courses to inspect for alignment, omissions, or redundancies. The program committee must ensure that over the entire $K-12$ program of studies learner outcomes satisfactorily address every program outcome for every content area. Figure 2.3 illustrates a matrix that may prove helpful in aligning program and learner outcomes.

This chapter has outlined the strategic planning process by which stakeholders' beliefs are transformed into learner exit outcomes and associated proficiencies. The program development process, through which program committees incorporate learner exit outcomes into in-

PROGRAM/LEARNER OUTCOME MATRIX

Grade Level:_____   Subject Area:_____

	PROGRAM OUTCOMES				
	# 1	# 2	# 3	# 4	# 5
Learner Outcome #1					
Learner Outcome #2					
Learner Outcome #3					
Learner Outcome #4					
Learner Outcome #5					
Learner Outcome #6					
Learner Outcome #7					
Learner Outcome #8					
Learner Outcome #9					

Figure 2.3 Sample program/learner outcome matrix.

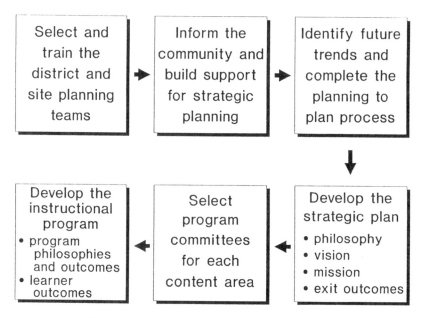

Figure 2.4 Steps in planning for authentic assessment.

creasingly specific levels of instruction, was also examined. Figure 2.4
summarizes the steps that comprise the strategic planning and program
development processes. Chapter 3 will describe development of authentic tasks—the basic units of instruction that comprise an authentic assessment system.

REVIEW ACTIVITIES

(*1*) What form of long-range planning is currently utilized in your
school district? How do various stakeholder groups throughout the
district participate in this planning process?
(*2*) Which specific groups and individuals from your school district
would you select to participate in the strategic planning process?
Why would you select each particular group and individual?
(*3*) Discuss some of the apparent advantages and disadvantages of
strategic planning compared to the planning process currently utilized in your school district.

(*4*) Articulate and discuss some of your personal beliefs regarding teaching, learning, and the role that parents and community members should play in the education of the districts' students.

(*5*) You have been requested by the district planning team to collect information regarding significant future trends that will likely affect your school district.
- Aside from the books listed in this chapter, what other media and information sources would you use to explore possible future trends?
- Aside from those listed in the Endnotes section of this chapter, what other future trends do you envision having a significant effect on the educational process in your district?

(*6*) You have been requested by the central office to assist in the identification of potential members to comprise program committees for the district.
- How many program committees do you feel would be needed for program development in your district? Which specific content areas would be represented by each of these committees?
- Who would you select to participate on each of these program committees?

(*7*) As a member of one of the program committees within the district, several parents and community members have complained to you that they want more direct input into program development decisions. How would you respond to these individuals?

ENDNOTES

1 Lyman, L. L. 1992. "Getting Results: Is Bona-Fide Strategic Planning More Effective?" *Educational Planning*, 8(3):31–35.

2 Herman, J. J. 1992. "Strategic Planning: Reasons for Failed Attempts," *Educational Planning*, 8(3):36.

3 Nebgen, M. 1991. "The Key to Success in Strategic Planning is Communication," *Educational Leadership*, 48(7):27.

4 Psencik, K. 1991. "Site Planning in a Strategic Context in Temple, Texas," *Educational Leadership*, 48(7):31.

5 Nebgen, M. 1991. "The Key to Success in Strategic Planning is Communication," *Educational Leadership*, 48(7):26.

6 A more detailed account of the planning-to-plan process may be found in Boschee, F. and M. A. Baron. 1993. *Outcome-Based Education: Developing Programs*

Through Strategic Planning. Lancaster, PA: Technomic Publishing Company, Inc., pp. 14–17.

7 Christensen, S. L. 1991. "Authentic Assessment: Straw Man or Prescription for Progress?" *School Psychology Quarterly,* 6:294–297.

8 For a more detailed description of the process for identifying future trends see Boschee, F. and M. A. Baron. 1993. *Outcome-Based Education: Developing Programs Through Strategic Planning.* Lancaster, PA: Technomic Publishing Company, Inc., pp. 17–22.

9 Barker, J. 1992. *Future Edge.* New York, NY: Morrow Publishing Company.

10 Boyett, J. and H. Conn. 1991. *Workplace 2000: The Revolution Shaping American Business.* Bergenfield, NJ: NAL-Dutton Publishing Company.

11 Celente, G. and T. Milton. 1991. *Trend Tracking: The System to Profit from Today's Trends.* New York, NY: Warner Books.

12 Cetron, M. 1985. *Schools of the Future.* Arlington, VA: American Association of School Administrators.

13 Naisbitt, J. 1994. *Global Paradox: The Bigger the World Economy, the More Powerful Its Smallest Players.* New York, NY: Morrow Publishing Company.

14 Naisbitt, J. and P. Aburdene. 1990. *Megatrends 2000: Ten New Directions for the 1990's.* New York, NY: Avon Books.

15 Schlechty, P. 1990. *Schools for the 21st Century.* San Francisco, CA: Jossey-Bass Publishers.

16 Toffler, A. 1990. *Powershift: Knowledge, Wealth, and Violence at the Edge of the 21st Century.* New York, NY: Bantam Books.

17 Future trends frequently mentioned include
  • increasing use of technology
  • increasingly rapid worldwide communication
  • increasing rate of knowledge acquisition and dissemination
  • changing family structure/disappearance of the two-parent nuclear family
  • increasing globalization and interdependence among all nations of the world
  • increasing cultural diversity
  • increasing expectations for higher quality products and services at reasonable prices
  • increasing concern regarding the global environment
  • changing political structures in Eastern Europe and around the world
  • shifting within developed countries from industrial-oriented to service-oriented economies

18 For a more detailed account of this phase of the strategic planning process see Boschee, F. and M. A. Baron. 1993. *Outcome-Based Education: Developing Programs Through Strategic Planning.* Lancaster, PA: Technomic Publishing Company, Inc., pp. 27–48.

19 Elements of the sample district philosophy were excerpted from a draft produced by the Rochester Public Schools, Rochester, MN, 1991.

20 This mission statement was developed by the Evergreen School District, Vancouver, WA.

21 This mission statement was developed by the Aurora Public Schools, Aurora, CO.

22 This mission statement was developed by the Rochester Public Schools, Rochester, MN.

23 Marzano, R. J. 1994. "Lessons from the Field About Outcome-Based Performance Assessment," *Educational Leadership,* 51(6):45.

24 The learner exit outcomes were developed by the Aurora Public Schools, Aurora, CO, and presented in Redding, N. 1992. "Assessing the Big Outcomes," *Educational Leadership,* 49(8):50.

25 A more detailed account of program committee formation and a program development model is presented in Boschee, F. and M. A. Baron. 1993. *Outcome-Based Education: Developing Programs Through Strategic Planning.* Lancaster, PA: Technomic Publishing Company, Inc., pp. 49–78.

26 This program philosophy was developed by Aurora Public Schools. 1992. "K–12 Content Outcomes," in *Pursuing Our Commitment to Life Long Learning in the Classroom, 4th ed.* Aurora, CO: Aurora Public Schools, p. 11.

27 These program outcomes were developed by Aurora Public Schools. 1992. "K–12 Content Outcomes," in *Pursuing Our Commitment to Life Long Learning in the Classroom, 4th ed.* Aurora, CO: Aurora Public Schools, p. 11.

28 Herman, J. L., P. R. Aschbacher, and L. Winters. 1992. *A Practical Guide to Alternative Assessment.* Alexandria, VA: Association for Supervision and Curriculum Development, pp. 26–30.

Chapter 3

ASSESSING INSTRUCTION

Authentic tasks provide the mileposts along the highway leading to the final destination of content mastery and learner exit outcome achievement.

Assessment of student progress toward established outcomes provides valuable information to those engaged in all aspects of the educational process. For example, information gained through quality assessment "helps educators set standards, create instructional pathways, motivate performance, provide diagnostic feedback, assess/evaluate progress, and communicate progress to others."[1] In contrast, "assessments that provide little substantive information and lack authenticity undermine the legitimacy . . . of the educational process itself. This can depress student learning, teacher commitment, and public support."[2]

Regardless of the particular purpose or format, quality assessments should meet certain common criteria. The Center for Research on Evaluation, Standards, and Student Testing (CRESST) recommends the following criteria for the assessment development process:[3]

- *consequences:* Does the assessment have positive consequences or are there potentially unintended side effects?
- *fairness:* Does the assessment take into account students' cultural backgrounds and their opportunity to learn the problem-solving and complex thinking skills on which the assessment focuses?
- *transfer:* To what extent do results on one form of assessment transfer to other tasks?

- *generalizability:* To what extent will assessment results support generalizations about student capability?
- *cognitive complexity:* Does the assessment require students to use complex thinking and problem-solving skills?
- *content quality:* Is the content selected for the assessment task representative of the best current understanding of the field?
- *content coverage:* Does the overall set of assessments cover the essential elements of the curriculum?
- *meaningfulness:* Do students find the assessment tasks realistic and meaningful?
- *cost and efficiency:* Is the information about students gathered by the assessment worth the time and effort required to obtain it?

Working within the framework of these criteria for a quality assessment system, learner outcomes must be translated into assessment tasks that provide direct evidence of progress toward eventual achievement of learner exit outcomes and program outcomes. The following questions should be addressed when designing assessment tasks[4]:

(*1*) Does the task match specific instructional intentions?

(*2*) Does the task adequately represent the content and skills you expect students to attain?

(*3*) Does the task enable students to demonstrate their progress and capabilities?

(*4*) Is the task authentic and does it simulate real-world tasks?

(*5*) Does the task lend itself to an interdisciplinary approach?

(*6*) Can the task be structured to provide measures of several goals?

DEVELOPING AUTHENTIC TASKS

Authentic tasks consist of student-centered activities that focus on real-world content and skills. While authentic tasks frequently involve the acquisition of knowledge and skills, their primary focus relates to the practical application of that knowledge and those skills. Since most authentic tasks require students to demonstrate a process or produce a product, they serve simultaneously as both instructional and assessment tools. Therefore, authentic tasks provide a direct link between instruction and assessment.

An authentic task[5]:

- includes concepts, generalizations, and processes critical to specific content areas
- is often interdisciplinary in nature
- requires a variety of information sources and gathering methods
- allows for multiple and varied products or outcomes
- provides maximum student control and regulation
- focuses on issues relevant to the student, the school, and the community
- provides opportunities for cooperation and collaboration
- is long term in nature
- requires the use of complex thinking processes

While some authentic tasks may incorporate all of these characteristics, due to practical considerations, most individual tasks will not. However, all authentic tasks should contain at least one of each of the following elements.

(*1*) *Learner outcomes* — clearly defined content knowledge and skills related to the topic being studied that students are expected to demonstrate through completion of the authentic task

(*2*) *Learner exit outcomes* — broad areas of knowledge, skills, or attitudes (with associated proficiencies), previously developed by the school district, that lend themselves to the learner outcomes identified for the task

(*3*) *Complex thinking processes* — higher-order thinking processes, as they relate to the topic being studied, that students will use to complete the authentic task. These processes, that are described in greater detail in Figure 3.1, include the following[6]:
- comparing
- classifying
- structural analysis
- supported induction
- supported deduction
- error analysis
- constructing support
- extending
- decision making
- investigation

Complex Thinking Processes	Key Questions Answered	Criteria for Evaluation
COMPARING: Articulating the similarities and differences between two or more items/elements on specific characteristics.	• Based on specific characteristics, how are these things alike or different?	• Did the student select appropriate items/elements to be compared? • Did the student select appropriate characteristics on which to compare the selected items/elements? • Was the student accurate in the assessment of the extent to which the identified items/elements possess or do not possess the identified characteristics? • Did the student come to a conclusion about the comparison?
CLASSIFYING: Organizing items/elements into categories based on specific characteristics.	• What groups can items/elements be put into? • Why are items/elements put into these groups?	• Were the items/elements identified for classification important to the topic? • Were the categories the student selected to organize the items/elements useful and important? • Were the defining characteristics of the categories useful and important? • Did the student accurately assess the extent to which each item/element possesses each defining characteristic?
STRUCTURAL ANALYSIS: Describing in detail the overall structure along with details relating to that structure.	• What is the critical theme, concept, or idea? • What details support this? • What information is irrelevant?	• Was the student accurate in the identification of the central structure, theme, or pattern? • Did the student accurately identify the structures subordinate to the central theme or structure? • Did the student accurately identify information not related to the central structure, theme, or pattern, or its supporting structures?

Figure 3.1 Complex thinking processes and how to evaluate them.

Complex Thinking Processes	Key Questions Answered	Criteria for Evaluation
SUPPORTED INDUCTION: Creating a generalization from information within the whole and then articulating that information along with the reasoning leading to the generalization.	• What conclusions or generalizations can be drawn from these specific instances?	• Were the specific pieces of information from which the student made inductions important to the general topic about which inductions were made? • Did the student understand the information or premises from which the inductions were made? • Did the conclusions (inductions) naturally follow from the specific pieces of information used to draw the conclusions?
SUPPORTED DEDUCTION: Identifying a generalization or an incident and then articulating the consequences of the generalization.	• What examples can I give of this generalization? • What has to be true given the validity of this principle?	• Did the student base the deduction on an important or useful generalization or governing principle? • Was the student accurate in the interpretation of the generalization or principle? • Were the conclusions drawn by the student logical consequences of the identified generalization or principle?
ERROR ANALYSIS: Identifying and articulating specific types of errors.	• What is wrong with this? • Why is it wrong? • How can it be corrected?	• Did the student select important or critical errors in the information or process? • Was the student accurate in the analysis of the manner and extent to which errors affect the information or process within which they exist? • Was the student's description about how to correct the errors valid?

Figure 3.1 (continued) Complex thinking processes and how to evaluate them.

45

Complex Thinking Processes	Key Questions Answered	Criteria for Evaluation
CONSTRUCTING SUPPORT: Developing a well-articulated argument for or against a specific claim.	• What is the issue? • What are the reasons for this argument? • What evidence supports or refutes claim? • What conclusions have you reached?	• Was the student accurate in the identification of information that needs support versus information that does not need support? • Was the student's claim supported by a sufficient amount and appropriate types of information? • Was the student accurate in the description of the limitations of the claim and the support provided?
EXTENDING: Identifying how the pattern within one piece of information is similar or different from the pattern within another piece of information and providing support for the reasoning leading to the relationship.	• What is the pattern in the information? • Where else does it apply?	• To what extent was the information identified from the original source important and useful as a subject for the abstraction process? • Did the abstract pattern the student identified represent the pattern of important information from the literal source? • To what extent did the related information contain the key characteristics of the abstract pattern?
DECISION MAKING: Choosing among alternatives which appear to be equal.	• What are the important criteria to use in making the decision? • Based on the specific criteria, which of the alternatives is best or worse?	• Did the student select appropriate and important alternatives to be considered? • Did the student select appropriate and important criteria with which to assess the identified alternatives? • Was the student accurate in the assessment of the extent to which the alternatives possess the identified characteristics? • Did the final selection adequately meet decision criteria and answer the initial decision question?

Figure 3.1 (continued) Complex thinking processes and how to evaluate them.

Complex Thinking Processes	Key Questions Answered	Criteria for Evaluation
INVESTIGATION: There are three basic types of investigation: **Definitive** – constructs a definition or description for a concept when this definition or description is not available or not accepted. **Historical** – constructs an explanation for some past event for which there is no definite explanation. **Projective** – makes a prediction about some future event.	• What are the defining characteristics (definitive)? • Why/how did this happen (historical)? • What would happen/would have happened if (projective)?	• Was the student accurate and complete in the assessment of what is already known or accepted about: ■ the concept (definitive)? ■ the past event (historical)? ■ the hypothetical event (projective)? • Was the student accurate and complete in the assessment of a confusion or contradiction about: ■ the concept (definitive)? ■ the past event (historical)? ■ the hypothetical event (projective)? • Was the resolution to the confusion/contradiction logical and plausible about: ■ the concept (definitive)? ■ the past event (historical)? ■ the hypothetical event (projective)?
SYSTEMS ANALYSIS: Identifying and describing the internal structure of a system, its operation, and how it interfaces with what lies outside the system.	• How does this operate? • What are the relationships between the components? • What effect does one part have on another?	• Did the student accurately and clearly identify the boundaries of the system? • Did the student accurately and completely identify and articulate how the component parts interact? • Did the student accurately and completely describe how the system can fail? • Did the student accurately describe how the system interfaces with the world outside it across the system boundaries?

Figure 3.1 (continued) Complex thinking processes and how to evaluate them.

47

Complex Thinking Processes	Key Questions Answered	Criteria for Evaluation
PROBLEM SOLVING: Developing, testing, and evaluating a method or product for overcoming an obstacle.	• What is the obstacle? • What are the alternatives? • Which alternative best overcomes the obstacle?	• Were the obstacles to the goal identified by the student? • Were the alternative ways of overcoming the obstacles identified by the student viable and important to the situation? • Did the student adequately try out a selected alternative before trying another? • If other alternatives were tried, how well did the student articulate the reasoning behind the order of the selection and the extent to which each alternative overcame the obstacles?
EXPERIMENTAL INQUIRY: Generating, testing, and evaluating the effectiveness of a theory to explain a phenomenon and then using those theories to predict future events.	• What is observable? • How can the observations be explained? • What predictions can be made from the observations? • How can the predictions be tested? • What are the results and generalizations?	• Did the student accurately explain the phenomenon using appropriate and accepted facts, concepts, and principles? • To what extent did the prediction made by the student logically follow from the student's explanation? • To what extent did the experiment truly test the prediction? • To what extent did the explanation of the outcome of the experiment adequately relate to the student's initial explanation?

Figure 3.1 (continued) Complex thinking processes and how to evaluate them.

48

Complex Thinking Processes	Key Questions Answered	Criteria for Evaluation
INVENTION: Developing a unique product or process which fulfills some expressed need.	• What needs to be improved? • What needs to be created? • What standards will be met? • What is the final product? • Does the final product meet the standards?	• To what extent would the invention proposed by the student improve upon the identified situation or meet the need that was identified? • How rigorous and important were the identified standards or criteria the final invention should meet? • How detailed and important were the revisions the student made on the initial model or draft? • To what extent did the final product meet the standards and criteria that had been identified?
COMBINATION TASKS: Analyzing or generating information via the explicit use of two or more of the previously described types of tasks or thinking processes.	• The specific question(s) answered are those related to the specific tasks or thinking processes being used.	• Criteria for evaluation are those related to the specific tasks or thinking processes being used.

Figure 3.1 (continued) Complex thinking processes and how to evaluate them.

- systems analysis
- problem solving
- experimental inquiry
- invention

Learner outcomes, learner exit outcomes, and complex thinking processes provide the basis for both developing the authentic task and assessing learner outcomes demonstrated during completion of the task. Procedures for assessing authentic tasks will be presented in the following section.

ASSESSING AUTHENTIC TASKS

Assessment of authentic tasks consists of various performance-based methods of measuring and reporting the degree to which students demonstrate significant learning results related to content and skills that are useful in real life. Authentic assessment uses outcomes from authentic tasks to determine how well students are achieving learner outcomes and utilizing complex thinking skills in the process of achieving these outcomes.

Authentic task designers should remember the following:

- Not *all* learning activities in the classroom have to be authentic tasks—more traditional instructional methods still prove valuable for developing some basic knowledge and skills.
- Authentic tasks should be utilized whenever possible regardless of the specific content knowledge and skills involved.
- *All* authentic tasks do not have to be assessed—some tasks may be employed primarily as instructional tools that are not formally assessed.

When creating authentic tasks for assessment purposes, the following guidelines will prove helpful[7]:

(1) Identify several important or relevant issues within the topic under study.

(2) Identify one or several learner outcomes for the task—that is, the specific content knowledge and skills students will demonstrate in completing the task.

(3) Identify the criteria (standards) that will be assessed for the selected

learner outcome(s). Focus on several important criteria rather than attempting to assess all the possible criteria for each outcome. In general, the criteria to be assessed for learner outcomes include the degree to which

- the student demonstrates understanding of the content area facts, concepts, and principles relevant to the task
- the student effectively used the content skills and processes relevant to the task

(4) Design a scoring rubric or performance scale to record the level of proficiency demonstrated for each learner outcome criterion. (Guidelines for designing scoring rubrics will be provided in the next section of this chapter.)

(5) Select one or two learner exit outcomes to incorporate into the task. Choose exit outcomes that particularly lend themselves to the knowledge and skills related to the topic under study. For each selected exit outcome, identify one or two exit outcome proficiencies that appear particularly relevant to the assessment task. (Due to the long-term nature of learner exit outcomes, it is not necessary to assess them in detail for every authentic task. However, assessment of student progress toward exit outcome achievement will be appropriate when making decisions regarding grade-level promotion or graduation.)

(6) Select one or two complex thinking processes to incorporate into the task. Avoid trying to assess too many processes for each task. Choose thinking processes that

- you would like students to learn or at which you would like them to become more proficient
- lend themselves particularly well to the knowledge and skills related to the specific topic under study

(7) Identify the criteria that will be assessed for each complex thinking process and design a scoring rubric or performance scale to record the level of achievement for each criterion. In general, you will be evaluating the degree to which the student utilized all of the important components of the thinking process necessary to complete the task. Suggested criteria to be assessed for each thinking process are summarized in Figure 3.1.

(8) Carefully review the authentic task that has been created to assure that

- the task will provide all the necessary information needed to assess the criteria that have been selected
- the task is meaningful and interesting enough to engage students and maintain their involvement

(9) If necessary, modify the task to ensure that it provides the necessary information for assessment purposes and is meaningful and interesting to students.

(10) Construct an assessment scoring sheet to be completed for the task that includes
- the topic students are studying
- the task students are to complete (and, if necessary, the conditions under which this should occur)
- learner outcome(s) selected for the task
- the criteria to be used for assessing the degree to which students have achieved the selected learner outcome(s) and a rating scale for recording results
- learner exit outcome(s) and exit outcome proficiencies selected for the task
- the criteria to be used for assessing the degree to which students have demonstrated the selected learner exit outcome proficiencies and a rating scale for recording results
- complex thinking skill(s) selected for the task
- the criteria to be used for assessing the degree to which students have utilized the complex thinking skill(s) and a rating scale for recording results

(11) If desired, assign differential weights to the selected criteria to reflect what students should emphasize in completing the task.

(12) Communicate clearly to students the criteria (and weights) selected for the task so they fully understand what is being emphasized in the assessment.

(13) Select an appropriate assessment tool/technique to measure or observe learner outcomes for the task (several sample assessment tools/techniques will be described later in this chapter).

(14) Guide students through the completion of the task and assess each student's performance using the assessment tool/technique you selected and the assessment scoring sheet you constructed.

(15) Upon completion of the task and assessment, share results with

students so that they understand how well they did, where their strengths and weaknesses were, and how they might improve on a similar task in the future.

Transitional authentic task development and assessment may be accomplished by selecting a project or activity that has been used previously and make it authentic by redesigning it in a fashion that adheres to steps outlined above. A sample generic authentic task assignment sheet is illustrated in Figure 3.2.[8] and a sample authentic task scoring sheet is illustrated in Figure 3.3.[9]

School districts should consider developing standardized formats for authentic tasks and scoring sheets. Standardized formats save classroom teachers valuable planning time, permit more time for developing the task content, and assist in recording observational and assessment data.

DESIGNING SCORING RUBRICS

As there are multiple ways to successfully complete performance-based authentic tasks, students' performance of the task must be judged by individuals guided by well-defined criteria. These criteria consist of scoring rubrics

> which consist of a fixed scale and a list of characteristics describing performance for each of the points on the scale. Because rubrics describe levels of performance, they provide important information to teachers, parents, and others interested in what students know and can do. Rubrics also *promote* learning by offering clear performance targets to students for agreed-upon results.[10]

Rubrics for Learner Outcomes

Scoring rubrics for learner outcomes provide descriptive criteria for judging the degree to which the student demonstrates (1) content-area facts, concepts, and principles, and (2) content skills and processes important to the specific task. For reliable assessment of learner outcomes, the proficiencies being measured must be clearly identified and the scoring rubrics must be designed specifically for the particular content and task being assessed.[11]

The following illustrates generic rubrics that could be adapted to

```
┌─────────────────────────────────────────────────────────────┐
│  ┌─────────────────────────────────────────────────────────┐ │
│  │ UNIT:                                                   │ │
│  └─────────────────────────────────────────────────────────┘ │
│  ┌─────────────────────────────────────────────────────────┐ │
│  │ TASK:                                                   │ │
│  │                                                         │ │
│  └─────────────────────────────────────────────────────────┘ │
└─────────────────────────────────────────────────────────────┘
```

LEARNER OUTCOME(S) (CONTENT)

Facts/Concepts/Principles:

Skills/Processes:

COMPLEX THINKING SKILLS

☐ Comparing
☐ Classifying
☐ Structural Analysis
☐ Supported Induction
☐ Supported Deduction
☐ Error Analysis
☐ Constructing Support
☐ Extending
☐ Decision Making
☐ Investigating
☐ Systems Analysis
☐ Problem Solving
☐ Experimental Inquiry
☐ Invention

LEARNER EXIT OUTCOMES & PROFICIENCIES

SELF-DIRECTED LEARNER
☐ sets priorities and achievable goals
☐ monitors and evaluates progress
☐ creates options for self
☐ assumes responsibility for actions
☐ creates a positive vision for self and future

COLLABORATIVE WORKER
☐ monitors own behavior as a group member
☐ assesses and manages group function
☐ demonstrates interactive communication
☐ demonstrates consideration for individual differences

COMPLEX THINKER
☐ uses variety of strategies for managing complex issues
☐ selects strategies appropriate to the resolution of
  complex issues and applies strategies accurately
☐ accesses and uses topic-relevant knowledge

QUALITY PRODUCER
☐ creates products which achieve their purpose
☐ creates products appropriate to the intended audience
☐ creates products which reflect craftsmanship
☐ uses appropriate resources/technology

COMMUNITY CONTRIBUTOR
☐ demonstrates knowledge about diverse communities
☐ takes action
☐ reflects on role as a community contributor

Figure 3.2 Sample authentic task assignment sheet.

AUTHENTIC TASK ASSESSMENT SHEET			
Criteria for Evaluation	Evaluation	Weight	Score
Understanding and use of topic-specific information:		1/3/5	
Did the student understand the content area facts, concepts, and principles important to the task?	1 2 3 4	_____	_____
Did the student effectively use the content skills and processes important to the task?	1 2 3 4	_____	_____
Use of the process of classification:			
Did the student use all important components of the process necessary to complete the task?	1 2 3 4	_____	_____
Were the elements identified for classification important to the topic?	1 2 3 4	_____	_____
Were the categories the student selected to organize the elements useful and important?	1 2 3 4	_____	_____
Were the defining characteristics of the categories important and useful?	1 2 3 4	_____	_____
Did the student accurately assess the extent to which each element possesses each defining characteristic?	1 2 3 4	_____	_____
OBSERVATIONS/COMMENTS:			
		OVERALL SCORE = _____	

Figure 3.3 *Sample of an authentic task scoring sheet.*

assess the content knowledge and skills for a particular learner outcome, and provides an example of how a general rubric could be adapted for a specific task.[12]

Facts, Concepts, and Principles (Content) Knowledge:

4 Demonstrates a thorough understanding of the generalizations, concepts, and facts specific to the task or situation and provides new insights into some aspect of this information.

3 Displays a complete and accurate understanding of the generalizations, concepts, and facts specific to the task or situation.

2 Displays an incomplete understanding of the generalizations, concepts, and facts specific to the task or situation.

1 Demonstrates severe misconceptions about the generalizations, concepts, and facts specific to the task or situation.

The following example illustrates how this generic rubric for content knowledge could be adapted to a specific learner outcome for fourth-grade mathematics.

OUTCOME: The student will demonstrate understanding of how basic geometric shapes are used in the planning of well-organized communities.

4 Demonstrates a thorough understanding of how basic geometric shapes are used in the planning of well-organized communities and provides new insights into some aspect of their use.

3 Displays a complete and accurate understanding of how basic geometric shapes are used in the planning of well-organized communities.

2 Displays an incomplete understanding of how basic geometric shapes are used in the planning of well-organized communities and has some notable misconceptions about their use.

1 Demonstrates severe misconceptions about how basic geometric shapes are used in the planning of well-organized communities.

Procedures (Content Skills):

4 Demonstrates mastery over the strategy or skill specific to the task or situation. Can perform the strategy or skill without error and with little or no conscious effort.

3 Carries out the strategy or skill specific to the task or situation without significant error.

2 Makes a number of errors when performing the strategy or skill specific to the task or situation but can complete a rough approximation of it.

1 Makes many critical errors when performing the strategy or skill specific to the task or situation.

Notice that each scoring rubric employs a four-point scale, with 4 representing the highest level of performance and 1 representing the lowest performance level. Educators from each district, school building, or classroom must decide what performance level will be considered acceptable. In the above sample rubrics, for example, a performance receiving a 3 would likely be the minimum acceptable level. While a 4 represents superior performance, a 1 or 2 fails to demonstrate sufficient mastery of the facts, concepts, principles, or content skills related to the specific task.

Rubrics for Complex Thinking Processes

Determining the degree to which students utilize complex thinking processes represents another component of authentic task assessment. Scoring rubrics for selected complex thinking processes provide descriptive criteria for judging the level of proficiency that students demonstrate in incorporating those thinking processes into completion of the assigned task. Reliable assessment of complex thinking processes depends upon designing a scoring rubric specific for the particular thinking process being assessed within the context of the authentic task.

The following illustrates an example of a scoring rubric that could be used with the evaluation criteria for the complex thinking process of comparing.[13] (Figure 3.1 presents evaluation criteria for all of the complex thinking processes.)

(a) Did the student select appropriate items/elements to be compared?

4 The student selected items that are well suited for addressing the objective outlined in the task description, and that show original or creative thinking.

3 The student selected items that provide a means for successfully addressing the objective outlined in the task description.

2 The student selected items that satisfy the basic requirements
of the task description, but create some difficulties for ex-
ecuting the task.

1 The student selected items that are inappropriate or that create insurmountable problems for the accomplishment of the
task objective.

Assessors would have to design a similar scoring rubric for each of
the other evaluation criteria associated with the comparing process.
They would also have to decide which proficiency level would represent
the minimal acceptable standard. (In this particular example, a 2 might
represent the minimum acceptable proficiency level.)

Rubrics for Learner Exit Outcomes

Learner exit outcomes describe in broad terms the knowledge, skills,
and attitudes students must demonstrate by the time they graduate.
Several proficiencies or performance indicators identified for each exit
outcome provide a basis for determining to what degree students have
achieved the broader exit outcomes.

Since learner exit outcomes represent cumulative achievement over
longer periods of time, they need only be assessed annually and prior to
graduation. However, scoring rubrics similar to those described for
learner outcomes and complex thinking processes still offer an excellent
vehicle for assessing learner exit outcome proficiencies.

A specific scoring rubric using descriptive criteria should be designed
for each exit outcome proficiency to enable reliable assessment of the
proficiency. The following illustrates an example of a scoring rubric for
the proficiency of *sets priorities and achievable goals* associated with
the learner exit outcome of *self-directed student*.[14]

4 Consistently develops clear, challenging expectations and goals;
has a clear sense of his/her own physical, mental and emotional
abilities, and strives to work close to the edge of competence;
perceives the value of goals and their accomplishment; shows
maturity of judgment in the establishment of priorities; establishes the criteria for success before beginning work.

3 Develops clear expectations and goals; realistically perceives own physical, mental and emotional abilities; finds value in goals and their achievement; establishes priorities before beginning any endeavor; establishes criteria for success before beginning work.

2 Does not reliably develop well-defined expectations and goals; sometimes unrealistic in perception of own physical, mental and emotional abilities; needs prompting to see value in the task; occasionally works without giving enough thought to priorities or criteria.

1 Seldom develops clear expectations, goals; rarely considers his/her own physical, mental and emotional limitations or abilities; has difficulty finding value in the task; rarely considers priorities or criteria.

DEVELOPING AUTHENTIC ASSESSMENT SYSTEMS

An authentic assessment system incorporates an assortment of assessment tools and techniques that conform to the principles of authentic assessment. Employing a variety of approaches to evaluate student achievement and progress greatly enhances the validity of the assessment process. A system that includes three different types of authentic assessments—multiple validations, student portfolios, and secured tasks—provides a wealth of information for assessing students' achievement and progress toward established outcomes.[15]

Multiple Validations

Multiple validations consist of a variety of authentic assessments made over time by many individual teachers and trained evaluators on the knowledge and skills considered important. While each validation addresses a discrete task or activity, over a long period of time the results of many such validations provide a cumulative profile of a student's progress toward established outcomes and goals. For example, over the course of a semester or academic year, performance scores derived from multiple validations would furnish one form of evidence for making decisions regarding student progress, grading, or promotion. Multiple validations include authentic tasks assessed through the following means:

- activity checklists
- concept mapping
- contracts
- culminating exhibitions
- hands-on demonstrations
- naturalistic observation
- oral interviews
- reflective journals
- writing assessments

Activity Checklists

A checklist consists of a list of behaviors or characteristics that an observer records when monitoring student performance. Frequently, the observer scores each behavior or characteristic with a *yes-no* rating by checking off those that are present or absent. As an alternative, a checklist may provide several levels of assessment that allow the rater to make more quantitative judgments. The teacher may use a checklist when observing individual students or groups and students may use checklists for peer assessments. Figure 3.4 illustrates a sample activity checklist that provides several assessment levels for each behavior being rated.

Concept Mapping

A concept map is a graph or drawing consisting of nodes that represent concepts or key terms connected by labeled lines. The lines denote a relationship between a pair of concepts and the label on each line describes the relationship between the two concepts. Completed concept maps furnish assessment information regarding the student's content knowledge and ability to construct or identify important relationships between terms and concepts within the content area.[16] Figure 3.5 illustrates a completed concept map.[17]

Essential steps involved in constructing a concept map include the following:[18]

(*1*) Select a set of concept terms.

	FREQUENCY			
BEHAVIORS:	1	2	3	4
Reads and follows directions				
Plans before beginning work				
Solicits input from others				
Shares information with others				
Works well with others in the group				
Uses a variety of problem-solving strategies				
Incorporates previous learning into solving present task				
Remains on task throughout the activity				
Uses a variety of thinking processes to find a solution				
Asks questions that are relevant to the task				
Justifies solution with relevant information				

Student Name   Person Rating

Activity   Date

1=Consistently   2=Frequently   3=Occasionally   4=Rarely

OBSERVATIONS/COMMENTS:

Figure 3.4 *Sample activity checklist.*

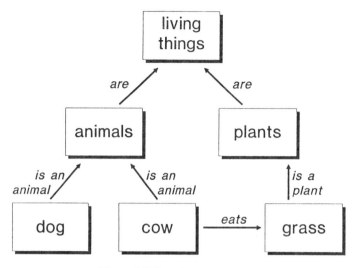

Figure 3.5 Sample concept map.

(2) Provide students with a sheet of paper and selected concept terms on 3 × 5 inch index cards.

(3) Have students sort through the cards and remove any cards containing terms unfamiliar to them.

(4) Students should then tape remaining concept cards onto the sheet of paper in an arrangement that makes sense to them, with the most related terms placed closest together.

(5) Students will draw lines between the terms that they consider to be related, then label each of the lines with the type of relationship they represent, and draw an arrowhead on each line to indicate the direction of the relationship.

(6) When completed, have students examine concept cards they removed in Step #3 and have them attempt to incorporate as many as possible into the concept map.

Concept mapping represents an extremely flexible authentic task that is adaptable to every grade level and content area. Through variations in the number of terms, complexity of relationships, and amount of information provided by the teacher, concept maps can supply valuable assessment data for a wide range of thinking processes and content proficiencies.

Contracts

A contract establishes academic expectations and responsibilities for the student entering into an agreement with the teacher for a particular task. The following basic elements should be specified by the contract:

- the specific task or activity to be completed by the student
- conditions under which the task will be completed
- the specific time frame for completion of the task
- what the final product or outcome will look like
- how the final product or outcome will be graded
- what resources will be made available to the student
- specific responsibilities of the student during completion of the task
- specific responsibilities of the teacher in assisting the student to complete the task
- procedures for changing any of the elements agreed to in the contract

Culminating Exhibitions

Culminating exhibitions or presentations provide students an opportunity to demonstrate that they have mastered the content knowledge and skills required for a particular task or project. Students make oral and/or written presentations to explain and defend the projects before a class or committee composed of teachers, other students, and invited community members. Assessment of the project and the presentation should include scoring rubrics or ratings for each of the following elements[19]:

- introduction to the presentation
  - gained attention of audience
  - established importance of subject matter
  - outlined objectives clearly
- subject matter included in the presentation
  - was practical and important
  - was accurate and complete
- adequacy of the presentation
  - selected and presented information and materials well
  - effectively used and organized information and materials
  - adequately explained information and materials

- performance was easy and smooth
- manner was pleasant and confident
- speech was clear and distinct
- teamwork and division of responsibility was evident (group presentation)
- results of the presentation
  - finished products or principles were developed
  - presentation had positive effect upon audience
  - summary was effective and accurate

Hands-On Demonstrations

Hands-on demonstrations afford students an opportunity to utilize manipulatives to display skills such as measuring, classifying, and technological skills. Hands-on demonstrations also provide a medium through which students can design and conduct experiments. Students may use demonstrations for formulating and testing hypotheses. Although traditionally reserved for use in the sciences, hands-on demonstrations are suitable for other content areas and for interdisciplinary activities. Assessment of hands-on demonstrations should include evaluation of the following criteria:

- appropriateness of hypotheses formulated
- accuracy of data collection and recording
- precision of data analysis
- logic of conclusions drawn
- understanding of the concepts involved
- real-world or practical application of concepts

Naturalistic Observation

Naturalistic observation, often called *kidwatching* by whole language teachers, consists of teachers observing individuals and groups "as teachers and students go about their daily work."[20] Teachers observe individual and group behaviors related to academic tasks, work habits, thinking processes, and other activities that influence student performance. The interaction among students in work situations and social settings provides an important focus for naturalistic observation.

Rather than complete a score sheet or checklist to document observations, teachers maintain anecdotal records that provide rich descriptions of what transpires among students as they work. Anecdotal records may also include descriptions of specific occurrences of events, as well as subjective impressions of how students interact within the context of the classroom environment.

Naturalistic observations provide valuable data for assessing behaviors related to learner exit outcomes such as student collaboration and communication. Many of these real-world skills prove difficult to assess using only scoring rubrics and quantitative data.

Oral Interviews

Oral interviews provide an effective technique for observing students' thinking and reasoning processes as well as their mastery of content material. Oral interviews range from very formal and structured to very unstructured and informal. Structured interviews, which require students to provide specific responses to focused questions, prove most useful for assessing specific content knowledge. In contrast, informal discussion of open-ended questions with an individual or group provides valuable evidence of each student's ability to think quickly, reason logically, and express his or her thoughts effectively.

Oral interviews furnish the teacher with an opportunity to assess students' depth of understanding rather than whether or not students can simply produce the right answer. Teachers have the added flexibility of determining whether an oral interview will be very brief or extend over a longer period of time.

The following presents suggested guidelines for using the oral interview as an assessment tool:

- Permit students to control the flow of the conversation—try to remain as neutral and unintrusive as possible.
- Encourage students to express themselves freely; remain attentive.
- Allow sufficient wait time to encourage students to think before they speak.
- Encourage elaboration of ideas by soliciting evidence or support for statements made.
- Encourage students to bring support materials with them to the interview.

- Encourage students to bring journals or logs with them to record the results of the conversation and their thoughts.
- Bring a notebook or pad on which you have jotted down important ideas to present and on which you can make notes regarding students' responses and conversations.

Reflective Journals

Reflective journals are notebooks in which students write about and respond to what they have learned, including questions and comments, and make notes of what they do not understand. Examples of what students may record in the journal include

- reflections about what they did or learned in a particular class or lesson
- feelings about a particular content area or course
- predictions regarding what they are going to learn in the next chapter, unit, or instructional cycle
- estimations of how well they are performing
- estimations of their level of effort in a particular class or on a specific task
- problems and/or questions they have for the teacher

Teachers may enhance the self-assessment value of reflective journals for students by providing probes. Probes consist of questions asked by the teacher to elicit responses related to a specific content topic, skill, or thinking process. In essence, probes provide the student a focal point for journal entries that the student can subsequently use for self-assessment purposes. The following illustrates several examples of probes:

- *content standard:* Describe the extent to which you understand the information about weather that we have covered. What information confuses you? How might you find out more about aspects of weather that interest you?
- *thinking process standard (classifying):* How effectively did you identify the critical characteristics for classifying geometric shapes? How might that information be useful to you in a real-world situation?

The teacher should meet individually with students periodically to examine and discuss their journal entries. This assists the student in using the journal for self-assessment and aids the teacher in assessing the student's thought processes and attitudes.

Writing Assessments

Writing assessments generally require students to write on topics assigned or suggested by the teacher. Their completed writing tasks are then rated by teams of readers who assign grades according to scoring rubrics or standardized criteria. Criteria commonly assessed on writing tasks include a student's ability to

- organize and communicate ideas
- construct sentences that are complete and varied in length and structure
- choose vocabulary words that most appropriately express thoughts and ideas
- construct sentences and paragraphs that are free from grammatical errors

Results of writing assessments provide information regarding students' content knowledge as well as their ability to express themselves effectively in a written format. Writing assessments also provide insight into students' reasoning and thought processes.

Student Portfolios

Portfolios consist of collections of students' work that provide tangible evidence of their knowledge, abilities, and academic progress in relation to established outcomes. Portfolios furnish students, teachers, and parents rich, authentic evidence of the student's performance capabilities and academic growth.

Benefits

When employed as an integral component of an overall assessment system, portfolios provide a number of benefits to students, educators, and parents. Some of the benefits realized through portfolio development and assessment include the following[21]:

- Most of the contents of the portfolio are actual pieces of the student's work rather than approximations provided by standardized test scores.
- Students have a vested interest in the creation of their portfolios – their tangible accomplishments generate much more ownership than files full of tests scores stored in the main office.
- When portfolios are part of ongoing classroom activity, the assessment is a model of the natural rhythm that learning takes in the real world. Assessment of the student's product is followed by a cycle of revision and assessment until a satisfactory final product is produced.
- Portfolio development and assessment are consistent with current learning theory regarding diversity in the pace and style of cognitive development among children. Due to the personalized nature of portfolios, they create an excellent structure for individualized learning.
- Portfolios require students to be active participants by making them partners in the development and assessment of their own work.

Purposes

Within an authentic assessment system, effectively designed portfolios serve various educational purposes. These purposes include

- assessing the quality of students' sustained work over varying periods of time
- assessing students' achievement of learner outcomes, program outcomes, and learner exit outcomes
- allowing students to showcase work that represents their own special interests and abilities
- documenting improvement of students' work
- encouraging the development and improvement of qualities such as pride in workmanship, ability to effectively self evaluate, and the ability to accomplish meaningful tasks

- providing a cumulative collection of work students may use in the future for applying to college and seeking employment

Contents of the Portfolio

Portfolio contents will be selected by the student and based on the student's expressed purpose for developing the portfolio. Important decisions regarding the contents and presentation of the portfolio should be made in collaboration with the student's mentor. Generally, the faculty or staff member who works most closely with the student will serve as the student's mentor. The mentor may be the student's content area teacher, homeroom teacher, team teacher, or member of the support staff such as a counselor or special needs teacher. If desired, a portfolio contract that establishes academic expectations and responsibilities for the student and mentor may be developed. Figure 3.6 illustrates a sample portfolio contract.[22]

Portfolios may represent a student's cumulative efforts over an extended period of time (a year or more) or focus on a more specific project or task. Cumulative (long-term) portfolios would likely contain documentation of the student's progress toward achievement of long-range program and exit outcomes, as well as evidence of achievement of more finite projects and tasks. A comprehensive portfolio will contain all the student's planning, research, and development documents, as well as the finished products. In contrast, a limited-focus portfolio will be more selective, containing only documents related to a specific project, content area, or limited time period. Documents and records that would appropriately comprise a portfolio include the following:

- traditional test results
- writing tests, essays, letters, and projects
- self-assessment documentation
- journal pages and entries
- sketches and drawings
- observational records
- anecdotal notes
- evidence of content area proficiency
- evidence of progress toward program outcomes and learner exit outcomes

```
                        PORTFOLIO CONTRACT

    This agreement is hereby entered into this _____ day of

    _____, 199___, between _____

    (the teacher) and _____ (the student).

    The parties hereby agree to the following:

        1.  The student shall provide all of the required informa-
    tion, skills, and effort needed to complete a portfolio that
    demonstrates _____

    _____

    _____.

        2.  The teacher agrees to assist, confer, and help the
    student in acquiring the needed materials, skills, space, and
    equipment.  And, the student agrees to make his/her needs known
    to the teacher so assistance can be given in a timely manner.

        3.  The student agrees to complete the portfolio for final
    presentation on or before _____, and at that time
    arrange with the teacher a date and time for presentation.  If
    the student is unable to complete the portfolio by the agreed
    upon time because of unavoidable causes, neglect by the teacher,
    or changes in the requirements for the portfolio, the student
    must negotiate with the teacher a new completion date and
    presentation time.

        4.  The student agrees to include in his/her portfolio the
    following information and evidence of work:

            a.  all necessary preliminary planning documents,
            b.  the initial representation--first draft--unedited,
            c.  evidence of responses and reactions of others,
            d.  evidence of revision and refinement, and
            e.  the final product and a plan for presentation,
                distribution, and/or display--logistics of time,
                place, space, and needed equipment.

        5.  All changes in the portfolio and work to be included
    within the portfolio must be negotiated with the teacher and
    and be in writing appended to this contract.  All additional
    work not specified in this contract, but deemed necessary to
    ensure a high quality of work, will be recognized and rewarded.

        6.  The student agrees to correct any and all work that
    does not conform to the specifications agreed upon in this
    contract in a timely fashion--not to exceed one week after
    the original due date and time.

    _____          _____
          Student                        Teacher
```

Figure 3.6 Sample contract for creating a portfolio.

- literacy milestones
- indicators of academic or social growth

Assessing the Portfolio

Periodic assessment of the portfolio should be conducted at predetermined times through collaborative agreement of the student and mentor. Depending on the purpose(s) for the portfolio, logical times for assessment might be at the conclusion of a task or project, the end of a grading period, semester or academic year, or toward the end of the senior year for graduation requirement purposes.

Portfolios provide formative assessment information that is useful for student self-assessment and assist the teacher in diagnosing specific problems and gauging student progress. Formative portfolio assessment will be relatively informal and consists of an individual meeting between the teacher(s) and student.

Summative portfolio assessment will be more formal and requires the student to make a presentation to a panel of judges. The judges will evaluate the portfolio and presentation according to a set of standardized criteria or scoring rubrics. The panel of judges should include

- two assigned teachers from different grade levels or content areas
- one teacher selected by the student
- one community member
- one other student

Although they will not participate in judging the portfolio, invited guests, including the student's parents, mentor, and peers, may also attend the presentation and examine the portfolio.

Reliable and uniform assessment of a portfolio requires the use of a specific set of criteria and scoring rubrics that indicate performance levels for key elements of the portfolio. Students must be apprised of these criteria in advance and judges must fully understand the significance of each criterion. Criteria for assessing the portfolio should include

- one or more meaningful purposes set by the student for use of the portfolio (for example, a specific task or project, graduation requirements, or college application)

- the degree to which the portfolio contents are quality products that correspond to the student's stated purpose(s)
- evidence in the portfolio of the student having demonstrated achievement of established purposes or outcomes (including mastery of relevant content material or proficiency of relevant complex thinking processes)
- effectiveness of the student's portfolio presentation to the panel of judges, that should include the degree to which the student
  - provides a rationale for the items included in the portfolio (based on the stated purpose of the portfolio)
  - communicates clearly and effectively

Figure 3.7 demonstrates an example of a generic scoring rubric for assessing a student portfolio.

Secured Tasks

Secured tasks consist of individual student performance under controlled conditions. Secured tasks include primarily paper-and-pencil tests, though they may also encompass simulations, in-basket exercises, and problem-solving activities completed individually.

Traditional paper-and-pencil tests, such as multiple choice, true-false, and short answer tests are examples of secured tasks. These kinds of tests provide powerful assessment tools for specific content questions because they are focused and efficient. For this reason, traditional paper-and-pencil tests should be used sparingly and limited to discrete content area assessments.

However, most paper-and-pencil tests differ from traditional tests in that they are open book and encourage students to make optimal use of available resource materials. These nontraditional paper-and-pencil tests are designed to measure higher-order thinking skills and the rational application of principles and concepts across content areas. Students are encouraged to apply and expand upon facts and concepts rather than simply provide memorized bits of information.

The following describe the main characteristics of secured tasks:

- Assessment tasks are administered under controlled conditions such as teacher-imposed time limits and specific directions for completion.

```
┌─────────────────────────────────────────────────────────────────────┐
│  ─────────────────────────        ─────────────────────────          │
│       Student's Name                    Judge's Name                   │
│                                                                        │
│  PURPOSE FOR THE PORTFOLIO:  _____          │
│                                                                        │
│  ESTABLISHMENT OF MEANINGFUL PURPOSE                                   │
│                                                                        │
│  4  Student sets well-defined purpose and provides a strong           │
│     rationale for this purpose                                         │
│  3  Student sets somewhat well-defined purpose and/or                 │
│     provides a reasonably strong rationale for this purpose           │
│  2  Student sets purpose that lacks clear definition and/or           │
│     provides a weak rationale for this purpose                        │
│  1  Student fails to establish purpose and/or fails to                │
│     provide a rationale for this purpose                              │
│                                                                        │
│  CONGRUENCE OF CONTENTS TO PURPOSE                                     │
│                                                                        │
│  4  Portfolio contents correspond extremely well to stated            │
│     purpose for the portfolio                                         │
│  3  Portfolio contents correspond reasonably well to stated           │
│     purpose for the portfolio                                         │
│  2  Portfolio contents correspond somewhat to stated purpose          │
│     for the portfolio                                                 │
│  1  Portfolio contents do not correspond at all to stated             │
│     purpose for the portfolio                                         │
│                                                                        │
│  ACHIEVEMENT OF ESTABLISHED OUTCOMES                                   │
│                                                                        │
│  4  Portfolio provides ample evidence that student has met or         │
│     exceeded all outcomes                                             │
│  3  Portfolio provides reasonable evidence that student has met       │
│     all outcomes or evidence is not clear for a few outcomes          │
│  2  Portfolio fails to provide clear evidence that student has        │
│     met all outcomes or evidence is lacking for many outcomes         │
│  1  Portfolio provides no evidence that student has met all           │
│     outcomes or evidence is lacking for most outcomes                 │
│                                                                        │
│  EFFECTIVENESS OF PRESENTATION--RATIONALE                             │
│                                                                        │
│  4  Student presents a clear rationale for inclusion of all           │
│     items contained in portfolio                                     │
│  3  Student presents a reasonable rationale for inclusion of all      │
│     items in portfolio or rationale lacking for very few items        │
│  2  Student fails to present a clear rationale for inclusion          │
│     of all items in portfolio or rationale lacking for many items     │
│  1  Student fails to present any rationale for inclusion of all       │
│     items in portfolio or rationale lacking for most items            │
│                                                                        │
│  EFFECTIVENESS OF PRESENTATION--COMMUNICATION                         │
│                                                                        │
│  4  Student communicates ideas clearly and effectively                │
│  3  Student communicates ideas well enough to be understood           │
│     most of the time                                                  │
│  2  Student fails to communicate ideas well enough to be              │
│     understood a majority of the time                                 │
│  1  Student fails to communicate ideas clearly enough to be           │
│     understood at all                                                 │
│                                                                        │
└─────────────────────────────────────────────────────────────────────┘
```

Figure 3.7 Sample portfolio assessment scoring sheet.

- Tasks are frequently assigned to assess specific content knowledge and/or skills.
- The precise content of the assessment is not known ahead of time (although the student may know what knowledge and/or skills will be assessed).
- Scoring is completed by trained assessors, including teachers or outside evaluators.
- Assessment of secured tasks closely matches learner (content) outcomes, suggesting that the assessment has content-related validity.
- Students are provided feedback on task performance and an opportunity to discuss assessment results.
- Secured tasks provide multiple opportunities for assessing promotion and/or graduation requirements and standards.

Since secured tasks consist largely of paper-and-pencil tests they are less authentic than portfolios or tasks used for multiple validations. However, assessment results from secured tasks provide valuable information for the parent, teacher, and student that supplement information obtained through other forms of assessment.

REVIEW ACTIVITIES

(*1*) What forms of student assessment are predominant within classrooms in your school or district? What form(s) of assessment do you personally rely upon most of the time?

(*2*) What form(s) of authentic assessment do you currently use in your classroom or school? What forms could you easily institute based upon your current assessment practices?

(*3*) What are some of the benefits of changing from a traditional assessment system to a more authentic system of assessment? What are some potential drawbacks?

(*4*) If you were placed in charge of a district-wide committee to implement authentic assessment, how would you convince other teachers to go along with you? Who would you want to be on your committee? Why?

(*5*) Portfolios have gained tremendous interest across the country for assessing student achievement. How would you integrate portfolio assessment into your classroom assessment practices? Would using portfolios be worth the extra effort it might take? Why or why not?

ENDNOTES

1 Herman, J. L., P. R. Aschbacher, and L. Winters. 1992. *A Practical Guide to Alternative Assessment.* Alexandria, VA: Association for Supervision and Curriculum Development, p. 2.

2 Archbald, D. A. and F. M. Newmann. 1988. *Beyond Standardized Testing: Assessing Authentic Achievement in The Secondary Schools.* Reston, VA: National Association of Secondary School Principals, p. 2.

3 Linn, R. L., E. L. Baker, and S. B. Dunbar. 1991. "Complex Performance-Based Assessment: Expectations and Validation Criteria," *Educational Researcher,* 20(8):15−23.

4 Herman, J. L., P. R. Aschbacher, and L. Winters. 1992. *A Practical Guide to Alternative Assessment.* Alexandria, VA: Association for Supervision and Curriculum Development, pp. 33−39.

5 This description of authentic tasks is based on a model developed by the Mid-continent Regional Educational Laboratory (McREL), Aurora, CO, 1991.

6 Descriptions of complex thinking processes, key questions answered, and criteria for evaluation were adapted from Marzano, R. J., D. J. Pickering, and J. McTighe. 1993. *Assessing Student Outcomes: Performance Assessment Using the Dimensions of Learning Model.* Aurora, CO: McREL Institute, pp. 67−105.

7 These guidelines are based on an authentic assessment model developed by the Mid-continent Regional Educational Laboratory (McREL), Aurora, CO, 1991.

8 Sample learner exit outcomes included in the assessment scoring sheet were developed by the Aurora Public Schools, Aurora, CO, and presented in Redding, N. 1992. "Assessing the Big Outcomes," *Educational Leadership,* 49(8):50.

9 Sample complex thinking skills and contents of the authentic task assessment sheet were adapted from Marzano, R. J., D. J. Pickering, and J. McTighe. 1993. *Assessing Student Outcomes: Performance Assessment Using the Dimensions of Learning Model.* Aurora, CO: McREL Institute, pp. 67−105.

10 Marzano, R. J., D. J. Pickering, and J. McTighe. 1993. *Assessing Student Outcomes: Performance Assessment Using the Dimensions of Learning Model.* Aurora, CO: McREL Institute, p. 29.

11 Marzano, R. J. 1994. "Lessons from the Field About Outcome-Based Performance Assessments," *Educational Leadership,* 51(6):44−50.

12 This scoring rubric for learner outcomes was adapted from Marzano, R. J., D. J. Pickering, and J. McTighe. 1993. *Assessing Student Outcomes: Performance Assessment Using the Dimensions of Learning Model.* Aurora, CO: McREL Institute, pp. 65−66.

13 This scoring rubric for complex thinking processes was adapted from a model developed by the Mid-continent Regional Educational Laboratory, (McREL) Aurora, CO, 1991.

14 This scoring rubric for a learner exit outcome proficiency was developed by the Aurora Public Schools. 1992. "Learner Outcomes Summative Rubrics," in *Pursuing Our Commitment to Life-Long Learning in the Classroom, 4th ed.*, Aurora, CO: Aurora Public Schools, p. 1.

15 The classification of authentic assessment techniques as multiple validations, portfolios, and secured tasks is based upon a model recommended by the Mid-continent Regional Educational Laboratory (McREL), Aurora, CO, 1991.

16 Shavelson, R. J., H. Lang, and B. Lewin. 1993. *On Concept Maps as Potential "Authentic" Assessments in Science.* Los Angeles, CA: National Center for Research on Evaluation, Standards, and Student Testing.

17 White, R. and R. Gunstone. 1992. *Probing Understanding.* New York, NY: Falmer Press, p. 18.

18 Concept mapping technique was adapted from White, R. and R. Gunstone. 1992. *Probing Understanding.* New York, NY: Falmer Press, pp. 17–18.

19 Scoring elements for culminating exhibitions were adapted from Boschee, F. and M. A. Baron. 1993. *Outcome-Based Education: Developing Programs Through Strategic Planning.* Lancaster, PA: Technomic Publishing Company, Inc., pp. 109, 111.

20 Marzano, R. J., D. J. Pickering, and J. McTighe. 1993. *Assessing Student Outcomes: Performance Assessment Using the Dimensions of Learning Model.* Aurora, CO: McREL Institute, p. 36.

21 Grady, E. 1992. *The Portfolio Approach to Assessment.* Bloomington, IN: Phi Delta Kappa Educational Foundation, pp. 12–14.

22 The sample portfolio contract was adapted from Boschee, F. and M. A. Baron. 1993. *Outcome-Based Education: Developing Programs Through Strategic Planning.* Lancaster, PA: Technomic Publishing Company, Inc., p. 110.

Chapter 4

ASSESSING STUDENT PROGRESS

As authentic instruction and assessment lead us into the Twenty-first Century, we must not permit grading and reporting of student progress to lag very far behind.

The transition from traditional instructional and grading practices to an authentic system of assessment represents a significant educational transformation. During this transition, classrooms are changing from a teacher-centered *testing culture,* where students work individually and learning is done for the test results, to a collaborative *assessment culture,* where assessment takes many forms, reaches multiple audiences, and distinctions between learning and assessment are blurred.[1] Therefore, as one educator involved in the change process observed, "the challenge remains for teachers—with the support of their districts, their professional organizations, and the educational measurement community—to devise grading systems that adequately reflect this change."[2]

ASSIGNING GRADES

Within an authentic assessment system, students are assigned grades based on demonstrated achievement of content area competencies identified by program outcomes and real-world proficiencies described by learner exit outcomes. Grades should reflect evidence of student achievement derived from multiple validations, portfolios, and secured tasks.[3] The relative contribution from each of these three forms of authentic assessments will depend greatly upon the specific purpose for assigning the grade (that is, interim progress reports, grade-level promotion, or completing graduation requirements). Evidence for grading provided by each type of authentic assessment may be summarized as follows:[4]

- *multiple validations* – a variety of authentic tasks that provide performance indicators regarding achievement of program (content) outcomes and learner exit outcomes
- *portfolios* – a collection of a student's work that provides cumulative indicators of achievement of program (content) outcomes and learner exit outcomes
- *secured tasks* – assessment of an individual student's work under controlled conditions that provide specific information regarding program (content) outcomes, but due to their specificity and focus, provide less useful information regarding broader learner exit outcomes

Regardless of the particular type of authentic assessment being graded, scoring rubrics similar to those previously described should be considered for assigning grades. Whereas traditional grades represent the average of many abstract numbers and scores, scoring rubrics provide grades that are descriptive of specific levels of performance. Grades represented by scoring rubrics are more meaningful to students because similar rubrics have been used to score the individual authentic tasks they complete throughout the grading period. The following generic scoring rubric, where a score of 2 would likely represent a minimum acceptable grade, illustrates how a four-point scale could be used to assign grades.

4 The student has exceeded the established standards (criteria) for that outcome.
3 The student has met all of the established standards (criteria) for that outcome.
2 The student has minimally met the established standards (criteria) for that outcome.
1 The student has failed to meet the established standards (criteria) for that outcome.

It must be remembered that such a scoring rubric is only meaningful within the context of the standards or criteria for each outcome. Therefore, clearly stated standards or criteria must accompany the grade received for the outcome.

The grade assigned for each program (content) outcome or learner exit outcome should reflect the student's overall level of performance in demonstrating the criteria or standards associated with each outcome. Averaging individual scores from multiple validations, portfolio assessments, and secured tasks provides a reasonable approximation of overall performance. However, grades representing an average value must be interpreted very carefully within the context of the individual assessments comprising the grades.

Interim Progress Reports

Interim progress reports consist of grades assigned to students' work at the end of a specified grading period, such as every six weeks, nine weeks, quarter, or semester. Interim grade assignment should reflect each student's demonstrated level of achievement and progress toward achieving program outcomes that relate only to the specific content knowledge and skills addressed during that grading period.

Multiple Validations

Each student must earn validations in every learner outcome assigned for completion during the grading period. The minimum acceptable score set by the school or district should be required for validation of *each* outcome. Prior to the end of the grading period, each student should be given the opportunity to demonstrate an acceptable level of achievement on any learner outcome for which validation is lacking.

A grade of 4 for the grading period indicates that the student earned the highest possible score on every validation (or, at least, most validations) completed throughout the period. In contrast, assignment of a 1 for the grading period indicates that the student failed to demonstrate an acceptable level of achievement on at least one or more validations. Grades of 2 or 3 represent acceptable achievement of all learner outcomes, but few, if any, scores of 4 during the grading period.

Portfolios

In conjunction with their teacher or mentor, students decide which materials in their portfolio they will present for assessment of each content area. Due to the potentially vast amount of material collected in all content areas during the grading period, it may be unreasonable to evaluate every content area every grading period. The following offer two alternatives:

(*1*) One possible approach would be to allow the student and mentor to decide on materials to be presented for only several content areas during any given grading period. By alternating content areas each grading period, the student will have been assessed on every content area during the course of the academic year.

(*2*) The second approach assumes that the school or district has identified one or more critical content areas that require more constant monitoring than other areas. Portfolio materials for these content areas (such as language arts and mathematics) could be assessed every grading period, while assessments of other content areas are alternated over grading periods throughout the entire year.

Scoring of portfolio presentations is based upon how well the student demonstrates achievement of all criteria comprising the scoring rubric(s) developed by the school or district. Results of both informal and formal portfolio assessments should determine the grade for the period.

Secured Tasks

Each student must receive acceptable scores on the secured tasks assigned for each content area addressed during the grading period. The level of performance constituting acceptable scores on secured tasks are determined by the school or district and incorporated into scoring rubrics used to assess the tasks. Whenever possible, prior to assigning the grade for the period, students should be given the opportunity to demonstrate an acceptable level of performance on all tasks done poorly the first time.

Grade-Level Promotion

Grade assignment at the end of the academic year for the purpose of promotion to the next grade level should also rely upon evidence of student achievement accumulated through all three types of authentic assessments. Final grades reflect student achievement and progress toward achieving all program (content) outcomes and learner exit outcomes made over the course of the year. Therefore, final grades should represent cumulative student accomplishments made throughout the entire year.

Unlike interim progress reports that focus primarily on achievement of content knowledge and skills, grades assigned at the end of the year should also document student progress toward achievement of broader learner exit outcomes. Proficiencies associated with each learner exit outcome should be assessed to provide information regarding exit outcome achievement.

Multiple Validations

Each student must earn validations in every learner outcome assigned for completion during the academic year. Whereas interim grades may address learner outcomes in only several content areas, final grades should report on progress across every content area (or, at least, every content area in which the student was enrolled over the course of the year). The minimum acceptable score set by the school or district should be required for validation of *each* outcome. Prior to the end of the academic year, each student should be given the opportunity to demonstrate an acceptable level of achievement on any learner outcomes for which validation is lacking.

Much like interim grading, a score of 4 for the academic year indicates that the student earned the highest possible score on every validation (or, at least, most validations) completed throughout the year. In contrast, assignment of a 1 for the academic year indicates that the student failed to demonstrate an acceptable level of achievement on at least one or more validations. Students demonstrating acceptable levels of achievement for all learner outcomes would be assigned a grade of 2 or 3 for the year.

Portfolios

Evidence from portfolio assessments accumulated during each interim grading period determines the contribution made to the final grade by portfolios. While portfolios may have been assessed during each interim grading period for certain critical content areas, portfolio presentations for other content areas will have been assessed during only one interim period during the year.

Determination of the final grade for portfolio presentations is based upon how well the student demonstrates achievement of all criteria comprising the scoring rubric(s) developed by the school or district. Results of both informal and formal portfolio assessments should determine the contribution made by portfolios to the overall grade for the academic year.

Secured Tasks

Each student must successfully complete at least one secured task within every content area covered during the academic year. However, due to the limited focus of many tasks, successful completion of various secured tasks may be required within certain content areas. On the other hand, depending on the nature of each student's instructional program, it is also possible that the student may be required to successfully complete secured tasks in selected content areas through agreement between the student and teacher or mentor.

The student should demonstrate successful completion of each secured task by scoring at or above the minimum acceptable level established by the school or district. Students failing to successfully complete all secured tasks during the course of the academic year should be provided an opportunity to demonstrate an acceptable level of performance on each unsuccessful task prior to the end of the year.

Progress Toward Learner Exit Outcomes

One element of each student's annual evaluation should indicate progress toward achieving the district's learner exit outcomes. While successful achievement of established proficiencies for all learner exit outcomes will be required for graduation, an annual progress report on proficiencies demonstrated throughout the academic year assist the student and teacher in identifying areas that will need attention during the coming academic year(s).

Grades assigned to indicate progress toward learner exit outcomes are based upon demonstrated achievement of those exit outcome proficiencies addressed during the academic year. Performance on scoring rubrics designed for each exit outcome proficiency provide information used to compute and assign grades.

Graduation Requirements

Requirements for graduation should reflect demonstrated proficiency throughout high school in all content areas, from achievement of program outcomes and attainment of all learner exit outcomes, to accomplishment of all exit outcome proficiencies. Evidence of content area proficiency should be based on authentic assessments that employ multiple validations, portfolios, and secured tasks. Multiple validations and portfolios should be utilized to provide evidence of accomplishment of all learner exit outcome proficiencies. Figure 4.1 illustrates an example of graduation requirements that specify

- which types of assessments will be utilized to provide evidence of achievement of program outcomes and learner exit outcomes
- the required minimum number of each type of assessment
- the minimum acceptable performance levels for each type of assessment[5]

Program Outcomes

Recommended procedures for assessing achievement of program outcomes for each content area include the following:

(*1*) *Multiple validations* – Each student must earn validations in every program outcome for each content area. The minimum number of validations required should be set by the school or district and should reflect the emphasis placed on each content area. A minimum acceptable score required for each validation also should be established by the school or district and will depend on the particular scoring rubrics designed to measure student performance.

(*2*) *Portfolios* – Each student's portfolio must contain tangible evidence of the student's achievements as they relate to each content area. Alternatively, through agreement with the mentor or teacher(s), students may select which content areas to include in the portfolio based on the student's stated purpose for the portfolio. Acceptable scores on portfolio contents and presentation should be established by the school or district.

(*3*) *Secured tasks* – Each student must successfully complete at least one

OUTCOMES	MULTIPLE VALIDATIONS	PORTFOLIOS	SECURED TASKS
PROGRAM OUTCOMES • Language Arts • Mathematics • Social Science • Science & Technology • Communication • Multicultural Issues • Environmental Issues • Career Management	The student must earn validations in every program outcome. Required: Score of 2 or better on every outcome.	The student selects which content areas to include based on the student's purpose for the portfolio.	The student must pass an assessment in each of the content areas. Required: Score of 2 or better on every outcome.
LEARNER EXIT OUTCOMES • Self-Directed Learner • Collaborative Worker • Complex Thinker • Quality Producer • Community Contributor	The student must earn at least 2 validations on each of the 19 proficiencies of the 5 learner exit outcomes. Required: Meet or exceed the District standard of 3 on each.	The student must include evidence of proficiency in all 5 learner exit outcomes. Required: Meet or exceed the District standard of 3 on each.	

Figure 4.1 Sample graduation requirements.

84

secured task in each of the content areas included in the student's program of studies. However, through agreement with the mentor or teacher(s), students may be required to complete more than one secured task in some content areas, or have the option of selecting specific content areas for task completion. The school or district should establish minimum acceptable levels of performance for successful completion of secured tasks.

Learner Exit Outcomes

Recommended procedures for assessing proficiencies for each exit outcome include the following:

(*1*) *Multiple validations* — Each student must earn a reasonable number of validations (determined by the school or district) on each of the exit outcome proficiencies. Scoring rubrics designed by the school or district for each specific exit outcome proficiency should be employed to assess students' performance levels. Descriptors comprising the scoring rubrics will determine the minimum acceptable performance level for validation of each proficiency.

(*2*) *Portfolios* — Each student must include in the portfolio evidence of achievement regarding each of the learner exit outcomes. Acceptable scores on portfolio contents and presentation for each learner exit outcome should be established by the school or district and based on the specific performance levels described by the scoring rubric(s) employed for portfolio assessment.

REPORTING GRADES

The transition from traditional instructional and grading practices to a performance-based system of authentic assessment necessitates a simultaneous transition to progress reports that accurately reflect student achievement and progress. For example, reflecting on the transition within her own school, one teacher observed, "we use a buildingwide set of rubrics to rate student progress on authentic tasks and assessments. There was just one glitch. Our instructional practice and the reporting system no longer matched."[6]

Preparing Stakeholders for the Transition

Properly preparing teachers, parents, and students is critical to the successful implementation of a new system of recording and reporting grades. School districts that are considering, or have begun the transition to performance-based authentic assessment should consider instituting the following key practices for orienting educational stakeholders.

Training Teachers

The reliability of the assessment process is greatly enhanced when teachers are trained to critically observe and interpret student behaviors in relation to established outcomes. In other words, when teachers are provided guided practice in rating student performance related to an outcome, they "better understand what children look like when they're achieving that particular outcome."[7]

One effective training approach consists of showing teachers videotapes of students being assessed, then having the teachers use established criteria to assign ratings to student performance. When teachers' ratings of the same performance disagree, they review the criteria and discuss the rationale for their own rating. Given sufficient time and practice, most teachers begin to internalize the criteria and rate student performances with increasing consistency.

Authentic assessment techniques generate much greater quantities of information to be processed than traditional fill-in-the-blank and multiple-choice tests. Therefore, efficient data management and record keeping represent another important focus for teacher training. Receiving instruction and ongoing support for using computers and available technology to manage data, keep records, and report results enables teachers to make a smooth transition to a new system of assessment and grading.

Communicating with Parents and Students

Parents and students represent the most important audiences for any newly developed system of reporting grades. Their genuine understanding and acceptance of the new progress report format provide the standard by which success of the transition will be judged.

Communication with parents must be established early during the transition and maintained throughout the process of developing the new reporting format. Parent meetings should be conducted by each school to explain the new progress reports, articulate the advantages of the new format, and address concerns raised by parents. Whenever possible, valid suggestions made by parents should be incorporated into the design of the new reporting format.

Most students should already be familiar with the new reporting format since a similar scoring system is used for judging their daily performances and products. They should be encouraged to interpret the new progress reports to their parents and explain how the grades appearing on the report were determined.

Piloting the newly developed progress report enables designers to "further refine the structure and wording as well as give [us] information about the best ways to introduce the new assessment process to administrators, teachers, students, and parents."[8] The pilot process consists of the following steps:

(*1*) Develop a prototype or draft of the progress report that is acceptable to all members of the committee designing the report.

(*2*) Conduct meetings with teachers, parents, and students to explain the new format and encourage questions and suggestions.

(*3*) Incorporating valid concerns and suggestions from teachers, parents, and students, produce a final draft of the progress report.

(*4*) When sent home for the first time, accompany the new progress report with an informational brochure and a survey to solicit feedback and suggestions from parents and students.

(*5*) Using feedback and suggestions from parent and student surveys, develop the final form of the progress report.

(*6*) Continue to monitor parent and student satisfaction with the progress report during its first year in use to decide if further revision will be necessary.

Designing the Progress Report

The primary purpose of a progress report is to clearly communicate expectations for students and "provide accurate and understandable descriptions of . . . what students have learned, what they can do, and whether their learning status is in line with expectations for that level."[9]

Within an authentic assessment system, this is accomplished by describing student performance in relation to established expectations or standards for program outcomes and learner exit outcomes.

Program Outcomes

One component of the progress report communicates student performance related to standards established for each content area of the student's program of study. Rather than assign a single grade to represent achievement for an entire content area, a grade is assigned for each program outcome identified for that content area. The grade represents the student's cumulative performance during the grading period based on evidence from multiple validations, portfolio assessments, and secured tasks. This provides students and their parents with a description of specific behaviors related to knowledge and skill development for each content area. Figure 4.2 illustrates a sample progress report that includes mathematics and science program outcomes.[10]

Learner Exit Outcomes

Consistent with authentic assessment practices, progress reports also describe student performance related to achievement of established learner exit outcomes. Grades are assigned for each proficiency associated with a particular learner exit outcome. The resulting report provides a profile of student performance on all the individual standards that, taken together, indicate successful achievement of the associated exit outcome. Figure 4.2 illustrates a sample progress report that also includes proficiencies associated with the *collaborative worker* and *quality producer* exit outcomes.

REVIEW ACTIVITIES

(*1*) What are the different types of assessments that teachers in your school district use to determine grades? Do they provide sufficient information for assigning grades that truly represent students' performance?

(*2*) What system for reporting grades is currently used within your

PROGRESS REPORT
Anytown School District
Hometown Elementary School

Student Name	Student ID	Year	Quarter	Grade	Teacher

PROGRAM OUTCOMES	QUARTER	1	2	3	4
MATHEMATICS					
Solves Problems ☺					
Uses Mathematical Language					
Recognizes and Creates Patterns					
Uses Probability and Statistics					
SCIENCE					
Knows How Systems Work					
Creates Models					
Interprets Natural Patterns					
Uses the Scientific Method					

LEARNER EXIT OUTCOMES	QUARTER	1	2	3	4
COLLABORATIVE WORKER					
Takes Charge of His/Her Behavior in Group					
Works with Group to Reach Goal					
Communicates Well with Others					
Shows Respect for Others					
QUALITY PRODUCER					
Makes a Product that Meets a Purpose					
Makes a Product for an Audience					
Makes a Product That is Well Done					
Uses Resources/Technology					

☺ = a proficiency that is scored every quarter

Figure 4.2 Sample progress report demonstrating two program outcomes and two learner exit outcomes.

school district? When was the last time that the system was revised or changed?

(3) If your district were to adopt some form of performance-based authentic assessment system, would your current progress reports still be adequate? If not, how would you change them to reflect the new system of instruction and assessment?

(4) How much training or inservice do teachers in your school district receive to help them better assess and report student achievement and progress? Would more training help teachers do a better job of assessing and reporting?

(5) How do you think parents of students in your school would react to a new system for reporting grades? What would the teachers at your school have to do to help parents through the transition to a new grade reporting system?

ENDNOTES

1 Kleinsasser, A., E. Horsch, and S. Tastad. 1992. "Walking the Talk: Moving from a Testing Culture to an Assessment Culture," Paper presented at the *Annual Meeting of the American Educational Research Association,* Atlanta.

2 Seeley, M. M. 1994. "The Mismatch Between Assessment and Grading," *Educational Leadership,* 52(2):6.

3 The use of assessment systems based upon multiple validations, portfolios, and secured tasks was recommended by the Mid-continent Regional Educational Laboratory (McREL), Aurora, CO, 1991.

4 Elements of the authentic grading system were developed by Aurora Public Schools. 1992. "Graduation Requirements," in *Pursuing Our Commitment to Life Long Learning in the Classroom,* 4th ed., Aurora, CO: Aurora Public Schools.

5 This example of graduation requirements was adapted from Aurora Public Schools. 1992. "Graduation Requirements," in *Pursuing Our Commitment to Life Long Learning in the Classroom, 4th ed.* Aurora, CO: Aurora Public Schools.

6 Kenney, E. and S. Perry. 1994. "Talking with Parents About Performance-Based Report Cards," *Educational Leadership,* 52(2):24.

7 Sperling, D. H. 1994. "Assessment and Reporting: A Natural Pair," *Educational Leadership,* 52(2):12.

8 Clarridge, P. B. and E. M. Whitaker. 1994. "Implementing a New Elementary Progress Report," *Educational Leadership,* 52(5):8.

9 Guskey, T. R. 1994. "Making the Grade: What Benefits Students?" *Educational Leadership,* 52(2):17.

10 This sample progress report was adapted from a model developed by the Clyde Miller Elementary School, Aurora, CO, and presented in Kenney, E. and S. Perry. 1994. "Talking with Parents about Performance-Based Report Cards," *Educational Leadership,* 52(2):24−27.

Chapter 5

ASSESSING THE CURRICULUM

"Any responsible conversation about assessment must attend to the quality of the curriculum." [1]

The story of achievement in America's classroom has two sides, one discouraging, the other hopeful. A measure of the public's attitudes shows that fewer people are giving the schools high performance marks, and more are saying schools are failing.[2] The American public perceives *fighting/violence/drugs, lack of discipline,* and *lack of proper financial support* as the areas of greatest concern. A smaller percentage perceived *standards/quality of education* and *poor curriculum and standards* as concerns. Contrarily, school board members, the nation's educational policymakers, identified *poor curriculum and standards* among the top three worries for education. This concern is preceded by *lack of proper financial support* and *state mandates.*[3] The common concern between the public and the educational policymakers is *lack of proper financial support,* which is number three on the public's list and number one for school board members. Sixty-seven percent of the people who deliver the curriculum to students on a daily basis, namely teachers, believe that they have no power to make significant curriculum changes.[4]

On the *hopeful* side are the five percentage point increase in mathematics achievement by fourth- and eighth-grade students over the past two years; an increase in the number of eleventh- and twelfth-grade students taking advanced placement examinations in English, mathematics, science, and history over the past three years; and an increase in the mean composite score on the American College Testing (ACT) program's assessment. On the international level, the United States' high school math team, composed entirely of public school students, won first place among sixty-nine countries in the Math Olympiad. The team math achievement resulted in the first perfect score in the history of the competition.[5]

ACHIEVEMENT BARRIERS

A number of research findings related to curriculum and instruction and standards should give the public and educators reason for alarm. A summary of the barriers to adequate achievement for many students include the following:

- In one major city, the teachers studied used forty-four percent of their class time for non-instructional activities. This was equal to the loss of two days per week of teaching time.
- A fifth grade in one school spent 140 minutes per day on reading while another fifth grade in the same school spent only sixty minutes on the same activity. This resulted in one fifth grade having 240 hours more reading time per year than the other.
- In a six-and-one-half hour elementary school day, students spent less than one-half of their time on actual instruction.
- The amount of time allocated by teachers to a specific area was as much as three times greater by one teacher than another (i.e., one teacher spent three times as much time on science or on the teaching of the Civil War as did another teacher).
- In a thirty-five hour high school week, students spent less than seventeen hours on instruction. The rest of the time was spent, among others, on announcements, passing out materials, waiting for instructions, assemblies, lavatory trips, lunch, and discipline.[6]

The aforementioned research findings should propagate an outcry from the public, school policymakers, and educators. Instead, we continue to ignore the findings. More alarming is the fact that professional educators in many schools do not understand the nature of curriculum, instruction, and standards and their relationship to academic achievement. If they do understand it, they do not practice it. There are, however, some things that our educational policymakers and educators can do to address the curriculum, instruction, and standards concern in a constructive way:

(*1*) Understand the profile of curriculum work: curriculum policy, fields of study, programs of study, courses of study, units of study, and lesson plans.

(*2*) Discern the six types of curricula: recommended, written, taught, supported, tested, and learned.

(*3*) Recognize the merits of the hidden curriculum and how it influences changes in student values, perceptions, and behaviors.

(*4*) Set in motion *curriculum mapping* as a technique to deal with the discrepancies between what might be in a curriculum guide, what teachers actually teach, how they teach it, and how they assess what is taught.

PROFILE OF CURRICULUM WORK[7]

The first concern for school policymakers, school administrators, and teachers is to understand the nature of curriculum and its relationship to instruction (see Figure 5.1). The connection between curriculum and instruction is defined as follows:

> The curriculum is the plans made for guiding learning in schools, usually represented in retrievable documents of several levels of generality, and the implementation of those plans in the classroom; those experiences take place in a learning environment that also influences what is learned.[8]

Curriculum, as defined above and in the broadest sense, includes both the plans for learning and the actual delivery of those plans (instruction).

Curriculum Policy

A board of education should have a curriculum policy that is a written statement specifying the rules, criteria, and guidelines intended to control curriculum development and implementation. For example, if a school board adopts the requirement that all high school students should learn about drug abuse, it is a part of the board's curriculum policy. If a

CURRICULUM POLICY

School board policy statement specifying the rules, criteria and guidelines for a district's curriculum.

▼

PROGRAM OF STUDY

All the fields of study supported by a school district. Examples are art, computer education, English/language arts*, foreign languages, health, home economics, industrial arts, mathematics, music, physical education, science, social studies, and vocational education.

*Language arts includes reading, writing, speaking, and listening.

▼

FIELD OF STUDY

One strand in the program of studies. Social studies is an example.

▼

COURSE OF STUDY

One course in the field of study, e.g. English I.

▼

UNIT OF STUDY

Subset from a course. The *Age of Exploration* in United States History is a unit of study.

▼

LESSON PLAN

Subset from a unit of study. Commercial Revolution could be a lesson from the *Age of Exploration* unit.

Figure 5.1 Levels of curriculum work.

school board requires four years of English but does not require any study of art, it has made an important value decision.

Program of Studies

A program of studies comprises the total learning experiences offered by a school district for its students. For example, a typical program of studies for an elementary school consists of reading and language arts (minimum of 800 minutes each week for grades one to three), mathematics (minimum of 250 minutes each week for grades one to three), social studies, health, science, art, music, and physical education.

The amount of time allotted to social studies, health, science, art, music, and physical education in grades one through three and to all subjects in grades four through eight is determined by program plans of study approved by the local school board.

The required fields of study within the program for the middle school and the junior high school are English/language arts, mathematics, science, social science, art, music, health, and physical education. For school accreditation, plans of study for the program must be approved by the local school board.

The units of credit required for high school graduation must include four units of English/language arts, three units of social studies, two units of mathematics, two units of laboratory science, one-half unit of laboratory computer studies, and one-half unit of fine arts. Some states require a unit in physical education. These requirements with electives (twenty units total) currently comprise a student's program of studies to graduate from high school.[9]

Field of Study

A field of study pertains to one strand in the total curriculum. For example, mathematics, $K - 12$, is a field of study.

Courses of Study

Courses of study are usually applicable to the secondary school setting; elementary educators tend not to think of courses. Courses are sets of organized learning experiences, offered over a specified period of time (a year, a semester, or a quarter). They are subsets within a program of studies and a field of study. For example, *second-grade mathematics* and *English I* are courses that students complete for credit.

Units of Study

Units of study are subsets from the various courses of study. They are planned sets of learning experiences organized as components of the courses of study. Units are usually organized around single overarching concepts. For example, a unit in a United States History course for grade eight could be *The Age of Exploration* or *The Colonization of the New World.* [10]

Lesson Plans

Lesson plans are subsets of units. The lessons usually focus on fewer objectives and should be geared to the time allotted to cover the material. For example, *Commercial Revolution* could be a lesson plan from the unit on *The Age of Exploration,* and *Spanish Settlements* could be a lesson plan from the unit on *The Colonization of the New World.*

FRAMEWORK OF CURRICULA [11]

The framework of curricula covers a broad territory, encompassing the recommended curriculum, the written curriculum, the taught curriculum, the supported curriculum, the tested curriculum, and the learned curriculum. To understand curricula (see Figure 5.2), it is important to know that the recommended curriculum, the written curriculum, the taught curriculum, the supported curriculum, and the tested curriculum are the driving forces for the learned curriculum and are considered the components of *intentional* curriculum.

When we use the term *curriculum,* we should include the entire content and nature of the educational program. The school curriculum, therefore, is not merely a number of courses, it is made up of human experiences. The school curriculum should offer to students rich life experiences that result in desirable knowledge, skills, attitudes, appreciations, and ideals. Thus, the intentional curriculum and hidden curriculum should be consciously planned and aligned in the curriculum development process. A good curriculum is a growing organism; it is never a finished product.

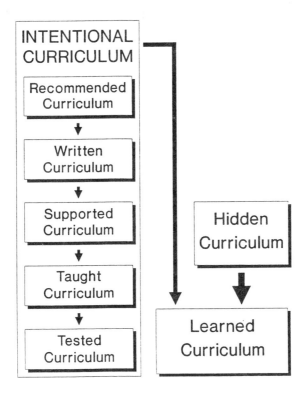

Figure 5.2 Curriculum alignment.

The Recommended Curricula

The recommended curricula (standards) for the fields of study by major professional and scholarly organizations[12] clearly identify what all students should know and be able to do to live and work in the Twenty-first Century. The standards are designed to be internationally competitive and address content and performance standards (see Figure 5.3).[13]

The content standards define what all students should know and be able to do. They describe the knowledge, skills, and understanding that students should have in order to attain high levels of competency in challenging subject areas.

The performance standards identify the levels of achievement in the subject matter set out in the content standards. They state how well students demonstrate their competency in a subject.

By high school graduation, students should know how
political institutions and religious freedom emerged
in the North American colonies. To do this, students should be able to demonstrate understanding of
how the roots of representative government and political rights were defined during the colonization
period by:

- comparing how early colonies were established and
  governed;

- analyzing fundamental principles of representative
  government in the colonies;

- explaining the development of representative institutions in the newly established colonies;

- analyzing how political rights were affected by
  gender, property ownership, religion, and legal
  status.

Figure 5.3 An example of a draft of U.S. History standard.

The national standards developed by the major professional and
scholarly organizations serve as a valuable resource for school districts
and states to develop classroom materials and lessons for a single subject
or combination of subjects. The standards will help school districts and
states revise their curricula framework to create coherence in educational practices by aligning instructional materials with assessment
practices. The focus is to ensure that the education system will provide
the opportunity for *all* students to reach high levels of learning. The
recommended standards should be perceived as *real,* not *ideal* for
curriculum development.

The Written Curriculum

The written curriculum consists of a school district's curriculum
guides, programs of studies booklets, and the scope-and-sequence
schemes. It should be an instrument that translates school district policies
and goals into documents that enable teachers to implement the district's
policies and meet the district's goals for learning. Written curricula for
the fields of study in a school district are essential, but often they are not
in harmony with what is taught.

The Taught Curriculum

"The taught curriculum is what teachers actually teach in the class-room." [14] If you were the supervisor and observed what is being taught, you should be able to recognize congruency between the written curriculum and the taught curriculum. Unfortunately, what is taught is sometimes quite different from the proposed written curriculum.

The Supported Curriculum

The supported curriculum is comprised of the resources provided by the district to support the intended curriculum. This includes "the staff, the time, the texts, the space, [and] the training." [15] To do a genuine evaluation of a field of study in a school district, the supported curriculum must be considered. For example, consideration must be given to the following questions: Is there adequate and qualified staff? How much time is allocated? Which textbooks are being used? Is classroom space adequate? How much staff development is provided?

The Tested Curriculum

The tested curriculum is the curriculum you see when you look at the instruments and/or activities used to measure learning. The tested curriculum is the measured curriculum.

The Learned Curriculum

The learned curriculum is the *bottom line* curriculum. It is what the students actually learned. (See Figure 1.1 in Chapter 1 on how to improve on the learned curriculum.) To maximize the learned curriculum, the written, the taught, the supported, and the tested curricula must be closely aligned.

THE HIDDEN CURRICULUM

The hidden curriculum consists of "those aspects of schooling, other than the intentional curriculum, that seem to produce changes in student values, perceptions, and behaviors." [16] Essential to having a balanced curriculum that is learner oriented, society oriented, and value oriented, we need to go back in history and recall some of the principles that John Dewey espoused nearly a century ago. Those principles, as applicable today as then, should be implemented to avoid shortchanging students and making curriculum for education an exercise in futility. The syntheses on the various topics that follow provide some insights for the hidden curriculum and are credited to John Dewey.[17]

The broad body of Dewey's work relates to the issues and, in many instances, provides solutions to the problems found in our public schools today. Yet, we seldom find educators drawing upon the principles and precepts developed by him.

Morality and the School

Among the educational concerns expressed by the American public, *lack of discipline* continues as the biggest problem facing public schools. Fighting/violence/gangs, lack of proper financial support, and drug abuse also rank high on the public's list of major problems.[18]

The public, as well as educators and school policymakers, have asked where the line should be drawn between the moral responsibility of the school and the moral responsibility of the home. Critics of education view the schools as doing nothing, or next to nothing, about moral deficiencies of public education, while educators claim that these are problems of the home and not the school. Neither side understands its respective function as it relates to the teaching of morality.

According to Dewey, no clear-cut line of demarcation exists between the responsibilities of the home and the school. The teacher needs to understand public opinion and the social order as much as the public needs to comprehend the nature of expert educational service. The business of both educator and parent is to see that the greatest possible number of ideas acquired by children and youth are attained in such a vital way that they become moving ideas and forces in the guidance of conduct. There cannot be two sets of ethical principles, one for life in the school and the other for life outside the school.

Rather than providing direct moral instruction (which would of necessity be comparatively small in amount and slight in influence), the implication by Dewey is that teachers should teach morals every moment of the day, five days a week, through their own characters, their methods of teaching, and the subject matter. School atmosphere and ideals should also reflect the whole field of moral growth. Because our society has established schools to do a specific work, Dewey claimed that the entire structure of the educational system in general needs to be considered periodically with reference to the social position and function of the schools.

Family structure has undergone rapid change in the past two decades. We can no longer assume that our youth will grow up in a traditional family setting where the nurturing influence of parents and relatives is constantly at work. "In addition, the shrinking of the extended family and decreased importance of neighborhoods contribute to limited contact between youths and positive adult role models." [19] In many of our neighborhoods today, young people are living in a *lockdown* situation (the grim lexicon of prison life) because the neighborhoods are unsafe. "While kids may need to be kept out of harm's way, there are physical and psychological drawbacks to growing up behind closed doors." [20] In reality, the neighborhood for many youth is not only the danger of violence but the absence of significant adults as role models. For youth from such neighborhoods especially, the last bastion for positive social interaction with other significant adults are the schools. The research on social interaction and school learning clearly states that

> . . . the connection to be made is between social interaction, in this case between teachers and adolescents, and cognitive development. Through relationships with adults the knowledge of the culture becomes validated. Adults in relationship with youths, often in informal settings, provide a structure for acquiring values and beliefs of society. These experiences contribute the basis for future experiences which provide the stimulation or food for cognitive growth. The formal knowledge of the culture is embodied in the school curriculum, where a student's success is often dependent on the extent of prior experiences in order to be able to do the work demanded in school. Consequently, social interaction contributes directly to the development of intellect. [21]

School policymakers and administrators must consider the significant implications of informal social interaction and cognitive development between teachers and students. If they do, "perhaps the movement to restructure will then become grounded in the value of social interactions with students not simply because of affective outcomes, but also because the quality of social interaction is a prerequisite for and an integral part of effective learning." [22]

Dewey proclaimed that moral motives are nothing more or less than social intelligence. The schools must, therefore, be agencies that provide: (1) a specialized learning environment that serves as a social institution in itself; (2) ways of learning and of doing work; and (3) the curriculum. Obviously, if these principles can be applied qualitatively, the schools will meet the basic ethical requirements, and the rest then remains between the teacher and the individual student, and the home and the child.

The Great Waste in Education

The most recent Gallup Poll conducted on the public's attitudes on the causes for increased violence in our nation's schools, "a breakdown in the American family (e.g., an increase in one-parent and dysfunctional families)" and "a school curriculum that is out of touch with the needs of today's students"[23] were, among others, consequential causes. An analysis of the two causes mentioned for increased violence in our public schools reveals that *the breakdown in the American family* should prod school policymakers and school officials to restructure the traditional six- or seven-period school day. Restructuring the school day for secondary school students would allow for informal and formal socialization between teachers and students. Concerning a "curriculum that is out of touch with the needs of today's students," the recent Gallup Youth Survey shows that "teens when given a choice say that their course work at high school should place greater emphasis upon such basic subjects as math, history, English, science, and foreign languages."[24] The Gallup Poll on adult opinions concur. Youth are also saying that geography, art, and music do not need more emphasis, according to the teen survey. With the exception of geography, adults coincide with the youth opinion poll (see Figure 5.4).

Dewey termed poor curriculum and low standards as "a great waste in education." His view was that a poor curriculum and low standards are caused by the inability of educators to capitalize on the experiences that youth get outside the school; students, on the other hand, are then unable to apply in daily life what they are learning in school. Dewey further believed the subject matter in elementary and secondary schools was full of facts that were not facts, and which would have to be unlearned later. Rather, Dewey stressed, students should learn what has real meaning—subject matter that enlarges the students' horizons. In

	YOUTH SURVEY			ADULT SURVEY		
	----Emphasis----			*----Emphasis----*		
	More %	Same %	Less %	More %	Same %	Less %
Mathematics	60	33	7	82	17	1
History/U.S. Government	54	40	6	62	31	7
English	50	40	10	79	19	2
Science	48	42	10	75	22	3
Foreign Languages	48	36	16	52	32	16
Geography	38	46	16	61	31	8
Art	37	43	20	29	46	25
Music	31	43	26	31	46	23

Figure 5.4 Gallup youth and adult survey comparisons.

light of this, students in our public schools today may be "information rich and action poor."

Dewey shared his thoughts about what a school curriculum should consist of in the 1915 edition of *The School and Society.* He implied that if education is to have any meaning for life, we must provide the student with the instruments that will give effective self-direction: active, expressive, and logical activities. It is the responsibility of our schools to introduce the youth of society into membership within a small community and to provide training so that they can later function in a larger competitive world.

Regaining Respect

Educators should know that "character education manifests itself in teacher practice as respect for each student as a responsible, active learner." [25] Students perceive model teachers as those who

- present clear, consistent, and sincere messages
- do not pull rank—are never authoritarian
- communicate high expectations
- really listen
- communicate their commitment through actions
- are hard-working and really care about student learning[26]

Additionally, the significant characteristics sought in teachers by students consist of "trust, honesty, high expectations, and caring." [27] Showing love is also an important characteristic when students characterize important teachers in their lives.

In his text *Experience and Education,* Dewey references quality teachers as "the organs through which pupils are brought into effective connection with the material." In contrast, however, we find that teachers, then and today, dominate the classroom with teacher talk, constructing only one educational activity that could possibly occur: listening, one mind dependent upon another. Dewey further emphasized that teaching and learning are correlative processes, as much as selling and buying. His analogy is that "One may as well say [s]he has sold when no one has bought, as to say that [s]he has taught when no one has learned."

The main objective of education, according to Dewey, is to prepare each student for future responsibility and for success in life. Traditional education has not allowed the students to experience school as a vital social institution; rather, it has presented subject matter as a finished product, allowing students no opportunity to participate in the growth, development, cooperative planning, and change which constitute the protoplasm of society.

CURRICULUM FOR THE WORKPLACE

School classrooms are *minisocieties* that replicate many structures of our larger society, including the workplace. It is through the presence of the seven curricula—recommended, written, taught, supported, tested, learned, and hidden—that students will be prepared for future responsibility and success in life. For students to be successful in the workplace, our public schools must consider the abilities that employers look for in their employees. The abilities are

- *learning to learn:* Employers are more frequently shifting employees between jobs and responsibilities, putting a premium on the ability to absorb, process, and apply new information quickly and effectively.
- *listening and oral communication:* Fifty-five percent of time spent in communicating is spent listening, but schools offer *scant instruction* in oral communication or listening.
- *competence in reading, writing, and computation:* Most employers today cannot compete successfully without a workforce that has sound basic academic skills. Although schools frequently teach isolated reading, writing, or computation skills, use of these skills on the job will require additional proficiency in summarizing information, monitoring one's own work, and using analytical and critical thinking skills.
- *adaptability (creative thinking and problem-solving skills):* An organization's ability to succeed depends on using creative thinking to solve problems and overcome barriers, thus placing a premium on workers who develop such skills.
- *personal management (self esteem, goal setting/motivation, and personal/career development):* Taking pride in work accomplished, setting goals and meeting them, and enhancing personal job skills to meet new challenges are necessary characteristics of employees. Unfortunately, the educational system provides little formal training.
- *group effectiveness (interpersonal skills, negotiation, and teamwork):* The ability to work cooperatively in teams becomes increasingly important for workplace success.
- *organizational effectiveness and leadership:* Employers want employees to have some sense of where the organization is headed and what they must do to make a contribution . . . and who can assume responsibility and motivate co-workers.

The seven abilities needed to be successful in the workplace are essential preparation for all students, including those going directly to work and those planning to pursue post-secondary education. In the broadest sense, the competencies are applicable from the shop floor to the executive suite. "They are the attributes that today's high performance employer seeks in tomorrow's employee." [28]

CURRICULUM MAPPING

Curriculum administration and assessment require specific information on such curriculum components as content and sequence, time frame, teaching methodology, and evaluation. Without such information, planning, coordination, resource allocation, and other decision-making activities are severely impaired. Besides, evaluation of the curriculum to determine a program's congruence with the school district's goals and objectives is difficult and infrequently undertaken. While curriculum guides provide readily available overviews of the desirable curriculum, they are often ambiguous, lack specificity, and do not represent the real curriculum. Curriculum mapping[29] formulates a procedure used to reveal the actual school curriculum. In essence, "curriculum maps reveal the real curriculum. Curriculum guides state what the curriculum should be. The curriculum guide is *prescriptive*. The curriculum map is *descriptive*." [30]

Curriculum mapping should be envisioned as a method to plot the taught curriculum. By comparing the collected data which consists of the content and sequence, time frame, teaching methodology, and evaluation, adjustments can be made to bring about better curriculum alignment.[31]

Curriculum Concerns

Curriculum should be a principal concern in education at all levels. Encompassing the objectives of instruction and the scope and sequence of content, curriculum should be the conceptual heart of the educational process in a school district for which all stakeholders are accountable. Implementation and administration of the curriculum and its components (i.e., course content and sequence, time frame, teaching methodologies, instructional materials, and evaluation methods) are perplexing tasks. Without specific information on these components, allocation of resources and other decision-making activities are severely impaired.

Using a thorough analysis of curriculum to determine if the education program in operation reflects the goals and objectives of the school district is an enormous task and is rarely undertaken. However, without curriculum analysis, no documentation of the actual program exists. While standardized test results may give some insight into overall effectiveness, they are not always available (many states give standardized tests to grades four, eight, and eleven) and they do not provide detailed information about the curriculum components. Local test scores may indicate how well students are meeting the internal requirements of the curriculum, not whether or not the curriculum meets the overall intentions of the school program. This requires a special mechanism for curriculum review.

MAPPING DIMENSIONS AND SAMPLE

The seven dimensions of a curriculum map consist of content and sequence, time frame, materials used, teaching methodology, organization of instruction, evaluation, and exit outcomes. The dimensions are built into the mapping scheme in Figure 5.5[32] and represent the components of curriculum mapping. The components are described as follows:

- *content:* Curriculum guides usually provide the content to be taught and the sequence in which the units are taught [*Written Curriculum*].
- *time frame:* Some curriculum guides indicate how much time should be spent on a unit or topic. In most instances the time frame is not stated [*Written Curriculum*].
- *materials used:* Many curriculum guides provide a list of sources (text, one source, or multiple sources) that can or should be used for a specific unit or topic [*Supported Curriculum*].
- *teaching methodology:* Very few curriculum guides, if any, specify how the content should be taught. In most instances, teachers have the autonomy to teach the content with whatever pedagogical method they choose and which is appropriate for student learning [*Taught Curriculum*].
- *organization of instruction:* Curriculum guides normally do not prescribe how instruction should be organized. Teachers can easily check how the class was organized on the curriculum map worksheet [*Taught Curriculum*].

- *evaluation(s):* Assessing the unit taught may or may not be found in a curriculum guide. If a form of evaluation is suggested, it is usually with secured tasks (teacher-made classroom tests, district-developed curriculum-referenced tests, and standardized unit tests) [*Tested Curriculum*].
- *exit outcomes and proficiencies:* Curriculum guides should indicate exit outcomes, the real-world knowledge, skills, and attitudes that students need to exhibit upon graduation. Curriculum guides also might indicate proficiencies, those measurable behaviors that indicate students are achieving the exit outcomes [*Written Curriculum*].

Although not all school districts have identified learner exit outcomes and proficiencies for their students, teachers should be able to assess if they addressed them in their classes. Examples of learner exit outcomes and proficiencies are illustrated in Figure 3.2. This information will be an asset for ensuring that students achieve the identified exit outcomes and proficiencies included in the district's written curriculum.

Mapping data can be gathered after each unit specified in the curriculum guide is taught. The sample curriculum mapping worksheet illustrated in Figure 5.5, shows the following.

Unit Taught

The Age of Exploration unit in the eighth-grade United States History course was the first of nine units in the study of cultural heritage from the Age of Discovery through the Civil War. The units that followed in sequential order were Colonization of the New World, The Establishment and Development of the Original Thirteen Colonies, Documents and Concepts of Our American Heritage, The American Revolution, Forming a New Nation, Changes in America, The Rise of Sectionalism, and The Civil War. Each of the units had several topics to be covered, listed in the curriculum guide. The instructional supervisor can easily see *if* teachers are following the written curriculum for the district [*Written Curriculum*].

Time Frame

Teachers can easily record the time when the unit was started and when it ended. If two or more teachers teach the same subject, a comparison

```
                    CURRICULUM MAPPING WORKSHEET

 ┌──────────────────────────────────────────────────────────────────┐
 │ Content and Sequence:                                              │
 │                                                                    │
 │    Subject: _____United States History_____    │
 │                                                                    │
 │    Grade: _____Eighth_____    │
 │                                                                    │
 │    Instructor: ____Any Teacher_____    │
 │                                                                    │
 │    Unit: _____I  Age of Exploration_____    │
 └──────────────────────────────────────────────────────────────────┘

 ┌──────────────────────────────────────────────────────────────────┐
 │ Time Frame:                                                        │
 │                                                                    │
 │    Semester or Quarter: ____One_____    │
 │                                                                    │
 │    Week/Day Started: _____One - September 5, 1995_____     │
 │                                                                    │
 │    Week/Day Ended: _____Three - September 15, 1995_____     │
 │                                                                    │
 │    Duration (instructional time): __Six hours_____     │
 └──────────────────────────────────────────────────────────────────┘

 ┌──────────────────────────────────────────────────────────────────┐
 │ Materials Used (list sources used):                                │
 │                                                                    │
 │    Text: _____America's Story_____     │
 │                                                                    │
 │    Sources (list): My Brother Sam is Dead; Across Five Aprils;     │
 │                    Slave Dancer; No Promises in the Wind_____      │
 └──────────────────────────────────────────────────────────────────┘

 ┌──────────────────────────────────────────────────────────────────┐
 │ Teaching Method(s) (check ☑ those used):                           │
 │                                                                    │
 │    ☐ Production-driven learning   ☑ Problem-based learning         │
 │                                                                    │
 │    ☐ Off-the-page learning        ☐ Reenactment learning          │
 │                                                                    │
 │    ☑ Technology and learning      ☑ Lecture                       │
 │                                                                    │
 │    ☑ Authentic research/learning  ☐ Other _____        │
 └──────────────────────────────────────────────────────────────────┘

 ┌──────────────────────────────────────────────────────────────────┐
 │ Organization of Instruction (check ☑ those used):                  │
 │    ☐ Large group   ☐ Small group   ☐ Individual   ☑ Combination    │
 └──────────────────────────────────────────────────────────────────┘

 ┌──────────────────────────────────────────────────────────────────┐
 │ Evaluation (check ☑ those used):                                   │
 │    ☑ Concept mapping   ☐ Contracts   ☐ Culminating exhibitions     │
 │                                                                    │
 │    ☐ Hands-on demonstrations   ☑ Naturalistic observations         │
 │                                                                    │
 │    ☐ Oral interviews   ☑ Portfolios   ☐ Reflective journals        │
 │                                                                    │
 │    ☑ Secured tasks ☑ Writing assessments ☐ Other: _____      │
 └──────────────────────────────────────────────────────────────────┘

 ┌──────────────────────────────────────────────────────────────────┐
 │ Exit Outcomes (check ☑ those addressed):                           │
 │                                                                    │
 │    ☐ Self-Directed Learner        ☑ Quality Producer              │
 │                                                                    │
 │    ☑ Collaborative Worker         ☐ Community Contributor          │
 │                                                                    │
 │    ☐ Complex Thinker                                               │
 │ Mapping date: ___9/15/95___   Instructor: _____Any Teacher_____   │
 └──────────────────────────────────────────────────────────────────┘
```

Figure 5.5 Curriculum mapping worksheet model.

109

can be made between or among the teachers teaching the units and the course [*Written Curriculum*].

Materials Used

The materials used should be recorded by the teachers. With the ever changing technology, some new material will be available that is not specified in the curriculum guide. Also, the instructional supervisor will know if teachers are using current material for some courses and if they are using sources other than the textbook [*Supported Curriculum*].

Teaching Methods

The teaching methods that teachers utilize to teach a unit should be identified on the "Curriculum Mapping Worksheet" (see Figure 5.5). Since the instructional supervisor cannot be in each classroom every day, this checklist provides information about what is happening in the classroom. The information may be most helpful in planning staff development for the school district or school. (For definitions of the teaching strategies used in the "Curriculum Mapping Worksheet," see the book by Boschee, F. and M. A. Baron. 1983. *Outcome-Based Education: Developing Programs Through Strategic Planning.* Lancaster, PA: Technomic Publishing Company, Inc., pp. 80−84.) [*Taught Curriculum.*]

Organization of Instruction

Teachers are given curricular materials such as textbooks, curriculum guides, and other supporting material to teach students. The organization of instruction and the way the material is taught—connecting the student with subject matter—is left entirely to the discretion of teachers. Providing information on *how* the class is organized will create an awareness for the teacher and help the instructional supervisor to know how teachers organize their classes [*Taught Curriculum*].

Evaluation

The types of measurement used to assess student learning can readily be identified by teachers and recognized by instructional supervisors on the "Curriculum Mapping Worksheet." This information is most valuable because it will show how teachers evaluate what is taught and assumingly learned. It is the *bottom line* (see Chapter 3 for elucidation of the various assessment techniques) [*Tested Curriculum*].

Learner Exit Outcomes and Proficiencies

Although not all school districts have identified learner exit outcomes and proficiencies for their students, teachers should be able to assess if they addressed them in their classes. Examples of learner exit outcomes and proficiencies are illustrated in Figure 3.2. This information will be an asset for ensuring that students are achieving the identified exit outcomes and proficiencies included in the district's written curriculum [*Written Curriculum*].

THE ALTERNATIVE TO CURRICULUM MAPPING

The alternative to curriculum mapping is status quo, business as usual. A recent curriculum-upgrading initiative that emphasized instruction by placing a premium on student understanding, problem solving, and an increasing control of their own learning failed. As shown in Figure 5.6, "over one-half of the instructional time was spent lecturing and reading (exposition) in both mathematics and science."[33]

Even though the state and university requirements were for lab work in science, a mere ten percent of science instructional time was spent in lab work and field work combined. In the student outcomes area, a heavy emphasis was placed on memorizing facts, understanding concepts, and completing routine procedures such as computation. "Virtually no time was spent involving mathematics students in data collection and data interpretation, and only 2 percent of time was spent involving them in solving novel problems."[34] In science, only ten percent of the time was spent on data collection and interpretation.

The findings of the study confirm that curriculum mapping is essential *if* curriculum reform and curriculum alignment are to become reality. Give teachers the tools to assess their performance and utilize the most from curriculum design, because teachers need uniformity, effectiveness, and organization for optimal efficiency. An inscription found on a seventeenth-century English church reads: "A vision without a task is a

Strategies and Outcomes	Mathematics	Science
Instructional Strategies		
Exposition	.562	.644
Pictorial Models	.079	.146
Concrete Models	.065	.048
Equations/Formulas	.237	.046
Graphs	.038	.014
Laboratory Work	.016	.095
Field Work	.000	.006
Expected Student Outcomes		
Memorizing Facts	.086	.310
Understanding	.295	.428
Collecting Data	.015	.078
Order/Estimation	.011	.050
Routine Procedures	.392	.022
Routine Problems	.148	.049
Interpreting Data	.023	.040
Novel Problems	.020	.017
Theory/Proof	.003	.003

Note: Numerical entries represent proportions of instructional time for a full school year and averaged over courses studied.

Figure 5.6 Average percentage of time spent on instructional strategies and expected student outcomes. Used with permission.

dream, a task without a vision is drudgery, a vision with a task is the hope of the world."

Curriculum mapping is a vision and a task that will strengthen written, taught, supported, tested, learned, and hidden curriculums. Curriculum provides an opportunity for documentation and evidence of accountability. Those who have a rigid reliance on the old paradigm of the textbook as the curriculum, and those who ignore curriculum components and curriculum mapping, mortify an effective school curriculum.

REVIEW ACTIVITIES

(*1*) To understand the main levels of curriculum work, draw a chart like Figure 5.1, indicating your school's curriculum policy, your program of studies, the field of study you are responsible for, courses of studies, and lesson plans that you teach.

(*2*) Provide an example for each of the six types of curricula: recommended, written, taught, supported, tested, and learned. What differentiates each type.

(*3*) Discuss how hidden curriculum influences changes in student values, perceptions, and behaviors.

(*4*) Map your curriculum. What discrepancies do you find between the curriculum guide and what is taught? What discrepancies do you find with what is actually taught? What discrepancies exist between what is taught and the curriculum guide? How do you assess what is taught?

ENDNOTES

1 Kohn, A. 1994. "Grading: The Issue Is Not How But Why," *Educational Leadership,* 52(2):40.

2 Elam, S. M., L. C. Rose and A. M. Gallup. 1994. "The 26th Annual Phi Delta Kappa Gallup Poll of the Public's Attitudes Toward the Public Schools," *Phi Delta Kappan,* 76(1):43.

3 National School Boards Association. 1994. "Common Measures," *Education Vital Signs,* (December):A18.

4 ———. 1994. "Common Measures," *Education Vital Signs,* (December):A13.

5 ———. 1994. "Common Measures," *Education Vital Signs,* (December):A11−13.

6 Minzey, J. D. and C. E. LeTarte. 1994. *Reforming Public Schools Through Community Education,* p. 81.

7 Permission was granted by the Association for Supervision and Curriculum Development and Dr. Alan A. Glatthorn to use the material on "Levels of Curriculum Work" and "Types of Curriculum" from the *Curriculum Renewal* textbook. Dr. Glatthorn is not only noted for his work in curriculum, he is a capable scholar, prolific author, and competent practitioner. For indepth insights on curriculum issues, see Glatthorn, A. A. 1987. *Curriculum Renewal.* Alexandria, VA: Association for Supervision and Curriculum Development, pp. 1–4.

8 Glatthorn, A. A. 1987. *Curriculum Renewal.* Alexandria, VA: Association for Supervision and Curriculum Development, p. 1.

9 The programs of study for the various grade levels and graduation are requirements for school accreditation for the state of South Dakota, and are excerpted from the South Dakota Department of Education and Cultural Affairs document entitled "Definition of Terms 24:03:01." Because education is a responsibility granted to the states, the programs of study for the various grade levels and graduation differ among the states.

10 Glatthorn, A. A. 1987. *Curriculum Leadership.* Glenview, IL: Scott, Foresman and Company, p. 17.

11 ——. 1987. *Curriculum Leadership.* Glenview, IL: Scott, Foresman and Company, p. 17.

12 Recommended sources for guidelines for the fields of study, K – 12, are as follows:
- *Art*
  National Art Education Association
  1916 Association Drive
  Reston, VA 22091
- *Business*
  National Business Education Association
  1914 Association Drive
  Reston, VA 22091
- *Civics and Government*
  Center for Civic Education
  5146 Douglas Fir Road
  Calabasas, CA 91302-1467
- *English-Language Arts*
  National Council of Teachers of English
  111 Kenyon Road
  Urbana, IL 61801
- *Foreign Language*
  American Council on the Teaching of Foreign Languages
  6 Executive Plaza
  Yonkers, NY 10701-6801
- *Geography*
  National Council for Geographic Education
  Geography Standards Project
  1145 17th Street
  Washington, DC 20036-4688
- *Health and Physical Education*
  American Alliance for Health, Physical Education, Recreation, and Dance
  1900 Association Drive
  Reston, VA 22091
- *History*
  National Center for History in the Schools at UCLA

231 Moore Hall, 405 Hilgard Avenue
Los Angeles, CA 90024
- *Home Economics*
American Home Economics Association
2010 Massachusetts Avenue NW
Washington, DC 20036
- *Mathematics*
The National Council of Teachers of Mathematics
1906 Association Drive
Reston, VA 22091
- *Music*
Music Educators National Conference
1806 Robert Fulton Drive
Reston, VA 22091
- *Reading*
International Reading Association
800 Barkdale Road
Box 8139
Newark, DE 19714
- *Science*
National Academy of Sciences
National Research Council
2101 Constitution Avenue NW
Washington, DC 20418
- *Social Studies*
National Council for the Social Studies
3501 Newark Street NW
Washington, DC 20016
- *Technology*
International Technology Education Association
1914 Association Drive
Reston, VA 22091
- *U.S. Department of Education*
For general information about content standards development, contact:
Office of Educational Research and Improvement/Standards
U.S. Department of Education
555 New Jersey Avenue NW
Washington, DC 20208-5573

13 U.S. Department of Education. September 1994. *High Standards for All Students.* Washington, DC: U.S. Department of Education, p. 4.

14 Glatthorn, A. A. 1987. *Curriculum Renewal.* Reston, VA: Association for Supervision and Curriculum Development, p. 3.

15 ———. 1987. *Curriculum Renewal.* Reston, VA: Association for Supervision and Curriculum Development, p. 4.

16 Glatthorn, A. A. *Curriculum Leadership.* Glenview, IL: Scott, Foresman and Company, p. 20.

17 See Boschee, F. and J. Schmoll. 1981. ''Solving Today's Educational Problems by Re-examining Yesterday's,'' *NASSP Bulletin,* 65(445):91–95.

18 Elam, S. M., L. C. Rose, and A. M. Gallup. 1994. ''The 26th Annual Phi Delta Gallup Poll of the Public's Attitudes Toward the Public Schools,'' *Phi Delta Kappan,* 76(1):43.

19 Galbo, J. J. 1994. "Teachers of Adolescents as Significant Adults and the Social Construction of Knowledge," *The High School Journal,* 78(1):40.

20 Marriott, M. 1995, January 23. "Living in 'Lockdown,' " *Newsweek,* p. 56.

21 Galbo, J. J. 1994. "Teachers of Adolescents as Significant Adults and the Social Construction of Knowledge," *The High School Journal,* 78(1):41.

22 ———. 1994. "Teachers of Adolescents as Significant Adults and the Social Construction of Knowledge," *The High School Journal,* 78(1):44.

23 Elam, S. M, L. C. Rose, and A. M. Gallup. 1994. "The 26th Annual Phi Delta Gallup Poll of the Public's Attitudes Toward the Public Schools," *Phi Delta Kappan,* 76(1):44.

24 Gallup, G., Jr. and A. M. Gallup. 1995. "Teens Want More Emphasis on Basic Subjects," *The Gallup Youth Survey* (Information provided by Robert Bezilla to be released to The Associated Press on February 15, 1995).

25 Williams, M. M. 1993. "Actions Speak Louder Than Words: What Students Think," *Educational Leadership,* 51(3):22.

26 ———. 1993. "Actions Speak Louder Than Words: What Students Think," *Educational Leadership,* 51(3):22

27 Galbo, J. J. 1994. "Teachers of Adolescents as Significant Adults and the Social Construction of Knowledge," *The High School Journal,* XXXX:42.

28 U.S. Department of Labor. 1991. *What Work Requires of Schools: A Scans Report for America 2000.* An executive summary prepared by the Secretary's Commission on Achieving Necessary Skills (SCANS), Washington, DC, pp. 1−6.

29 English, F. W. 1978. *Quality Control in Curriculum Development.* Arlington, VA: American Association of School Administrators.

30 ———. 1987. *Curriculum Management for Schools • Colleges • Business.* Springfield, IL: Charles C. Thomas, Publisher, p. 211.

31 ———. 1987. *Curriculum Management for Schools • Colleges • Business.* Springfield, IL: Charles C. Thomas, Publisher, p. 211.

32 Adapted from a curriculum mapping worksheet illustrated by English, F. W. 1978. *Quality Control In Curriculum Development.* Arlington, VA: American Association of School Administrators, pp. 36−39.

33 Porter, A. C., J. Smithson and E. Osthoff. 1994. "Standard Setting as a Strategy for Upgrading High School Mathematics and Science," in *The Governance of Curriculum,* R. F. Elmore and S. H. Fuhrman, eds. Alexandria, VA: Association for Supervision and Curriculum Development, pp. 159−160.

34 ———. 1994. "Standard Setting as a Strategy for Upgrading High School Mathematics and Science," in *The Governance of Curriculum,* R. F. Elmore and S. H. Fuhrman. eds. Alexandria, VA: Association for Supervision and Curriculum Development, p. 160.

Chapter 6

ASSESSING SCHOOL GOVERNANCE AND EFFECTIVE SCHOOLS

"Them that's going, get in the . . . wagon. Them that ain't, get out of the . . . way."
—from The Bear *by William Faulkner*

From birth we face a succession of developmental tasks as we learn to coordinate our different body systems. Focusing our eyes, coordinating our hands and eyes, walking, and riding a bicycle all involve fairly simple physical skills, but learning to integrate those skills into a coordinated whole is a major learning accomplishment.[1] Similarly, concerns for educational reform today include those of coordination. It is not right to just blame the schools for being ineffective; rather, one must consider all the entities responsible for educating its youth. This responsibility resides within the boundaries of each state because the powers of the federal government are circumscribed by delegation within the United States Constitution, Amendment X, which states that "The powers not delegated to the United States by the Constitution, nor prohibited by it to the States, are reserved to the States respectively, or to the people."[2]

As such, the responsibility for education is reserved to the states or to the people. Subsequently, states specifically address their obligation to education in their constitutions. For example, Article VIII, Section 1 of the Uniform System of Free Public Schools, in the South Dakota Constitution states the following:

> The stability of a republican form of government depending on the morality and intelligence of the people, it shall be the duty of the Legislature to establish and maintain a general and uniform system of

117

public schools wherein tuition shall be without charge, and equally open to all; and to adopt all suitable means to secure to the people the advantages and opportunities of education.[3]

Since public education is a governmental function belonging to the states, it is their duty to maintain educational standards by legislation, by administrative supervision, and by appropriation. The legislative body in each state has the right to create, organize and reorganize school districts, set the guidelines for employing and dismissing personnel, prescribe curriculum, establish and enforce accreditation standards, and govern all management and operation functions of the public schools.

The states carry out their educational functions through

- state boards of education, whose members are appointed by the Governor of that state with the advice and consent of the State Senate or elected by the people; who through their rule-making function, establish certification requirements, determine which subjects, and how much of each, are taught in the public schools, and institute guidelines for the physical environment for the teaching and learning processes
- state superintendents of public instruction (chosen by popular vote, by appointment of the governor, or by selection of the state board of education) whose primary responsibility is general supervision over all elementary and secondary schools subject to the policies set forth by the state board of education
- local school boards, elected in most states to serve as the governing boards of school districts for the purpose of organizing, maintaining, and establishing schools for providing educational opportunities and services for all citizens residing within the school districts

Local school boards have no common law powers; they are creatures of the state legislature. Their function is to carry into effect the will of the state as expressed by the legislature. Subsequently, school boards are the administrative bodies for their school districts, and have strict limited legislative responsibility and broad administrative power.

POWERS AND DUTIES

While separate entities responsible for education at the state level may be doing their jobs as they understand them, all too often their efforts, for one reason or another, are not aligned. As illustrated in Figure 6.1,

```
┌─────────────────────────────────────────────────────────────┐
│  ┌───────────────────────────────────────────────────────┐  │
│  │              PEOPLE OF THE WHOLE STATE                 │  │
│  │                                                       │  │
│  │   Elect a state legislature which enacts laws         │  │
│  │   governing the schools in every school district      │  │
│  │   of the state                                        │  │
│  └───────────────────────────────────────────────────────┘  │
│                            ▼                                 │
│  ┌───────────────────────────────────────────────────────┐  │
│  │            PEOPLE OF THE SCHOOL DISTRICT               │  │
│  │                                                       │  │
│  │   Provide a school board to operate the schools of    │  │
│  │   district and appraise the work of the board at      │  │
│  │   regular elections                                   │  │
│  └───────────────────────────────────────────────────────┘  │
│                            ▼                                 │
│  ┌───────────────────────────────────────────────────────┐  │
│  │                    SCHOOL BOARD                        │  │
│  │                                                       │  │
│  │   Adopts school policies; selects a superintendent    │  │
│  │   of schools and delegates to him/her the execution   │  │
│  │   of school policies; appraises the working of the    │  │
│  │   policies and makes changes in them as needed        │  │
│  └───────────────────────────────────────────────────────┘  │
│                            ▼                                 │
│  ┌───────────────────────────────────────────────────────┐  │
│  │                SUPERINTENDENT OF SCHOOLS               │  │
│  │                                                       │  │
│  │   Acts as chief executive of the school system;       │  │
│  │   makes recommendations to the school board; keeps    │  │
│  │   the board, school employees, and people informed    │  │
│  │   of conditions in the schools; furnishes educa-      │  │
│  │   tional leadership to the board, school employees    │  │
│  │   and community                                       │  │
│  └───────────────────────────────────────────────────────┘  │
│                            ▼                                 │
│  ┌───────────────────────────────────────────────────────┐  │
│  │                      PRINCIPALS                        │  │
│  │                                                       │  │
│  │   Supervise and administer individual schools;        │  │
│  │   delegate to teachers classroom instruction;         │  │
│  │   appraise the work of the teachers; keep the         │  │
│  │   superintendent informed regarding the work of       │  │
│  │   the school                                          │  │
│  └───────────────────────────────────────────────────────┘  │
│              ▼                          ▼                    │
│  ┌────────────────────┐   ┌─────────────────────────────┐   │
│  │      TEACHERS      │   │    NONCERTIFIED EMPLOYEES    │   │
│  │                    │   │                             │   │
│  │      Instruct      │   │        Facilitate the       │   │
│  │        the         │   │       instruction of        │   │
│  │      students      │   │      students through       │   │
│  │                    │   │       care of the school    │   │
│  │                    │   │       plant and other       │   │
│  │                    │   │            duties           │   │
│  └────────────────────┘   └─────────────────────────────┘   │
└─────────────────────────────────────────────────────────────┘
```

Figure 6.1 *General outline of the powers and duties of the people, local officials, and employees.*

the people in the states have the major responsibility of electing a state legislature which establishes the laws governing the public schools in their state.

In most school districts, the people have the right to elect school board members to operate the schools in the district. In turn, the school boards have the responsibility to make school district policies and select administrators (in most states) to enforce those policies. This sequence of responsibility is followed by principals who supervise and administer the schools, by teachers who instruct the students, and other non-certified employees who facilitate the instruction and activities in schools through care of the school buildings and other duties.

The question of who makes the educational decisions for our public schools is a fundamental and timeless issue which has received continuing discussion and debate since the United States Constitution was framed. Answers to this question have changed over time and are certain to change in the future, given the increasing rate and complexity of change in the United States and in the world. It is one of those fundamental questions that will always need to be reconsidered as new social contexts, pressures, and knowledge come to bear upon it. The array of participants who are officially designated or who function through default to make educational decisions is complex enough, but the question centers around not only *who* makes them, but also what type of educational decision is under discussion. Thus, the question is very complex and multifaceted, but the complexity is not often recognized when debates about educational reform and effective schools are held in public and educational forums and when operational answers to it are formulated.[4]

ASSESSMENT OF EDUCATIONAL REFORM AND FAILURE

The ebb and flow of school reform in the United States has particularly increased since the mid-1950s. The result has been that

> . . . each effort has left its mark, or scars; but few survived and most left a patchwork of programs, a host of disillusioned and jaded teachers and administrators, and a cynical and distrusting public cautious about investing in new educational ventures.[5]

The struggle over educational reform has been portrayed by some as an equity versus excellence issue. Others have looked outside the educational system for the answer and concluded that "throughout its history this country has lurched from crisis to crisis, and so the mere emergence of another difficult period, as now exists, may not be particularly remarkable or perhaps even worrisome."[6]

Various attempts have been made to reform the educational system in the United States during the last decade. A recent study[7] on why education reforms failed discloses that (a) lack of agreed purpose, (b) lack of direction, and (c) lack of commitment are the three basic reasons. Each of the reasons provides a reliable compass for understanding what may continue to hamper educational reform.

Lack of Agreed Purpose

Lack of agreed purpose was the key problem in explaining the failure of educational reform during the decade from 1983 – 1993. The characteristics of *lack of agreed purpose* are as follows:

- disagreement over reform proposals
- disagreement over purpose of public education
- disagreement over the terms: *reform, failure,* and *restructuring*
- conflicting waves of reform
- reform as media event, rhetoric, or political hype
- proponents conflicting over best methods of improving public education
- excellence versus equity argument
- top-down control, empowerment, bottom-up, collaboration, and grass roots all undefined
- fads and media reports without basis in research; a crisis atmosphere
- lack of effective leadership related to lack of agreed purpose[8]

The research literature, consisting of primary and secondary references, discloses that *lack of agreed purpose* was the most oft-cited response for explaining reform failure. Educational reform experts, politicians, educators, and researchers were in agreement that the reform movement for schools had no real purpose.

Lack of Direction

The lack of a federal goal for education, a lack of similar goals for most states, and a lack of agreement are the major contributing factors for *lack of direction,* which is a cause of educational reform failure. The characteristics of *lack of direction* are

- lack of a federal goal for education
- no overall federal leadership
- each state controlling its own educational system
- lack of state goals for education
- local school boards; each district is independent
- lack of a vision for education
- hidden agenda, no nationally agreed-upon direction

The inability to have a vision and to set a proper course for educational reform was evident for the failure of educational reform. To have a federal system of government with state control of education along with thousands of school boards mitigates against having a clear direction for education. The configuration is analogous to a boat filled with people who are rowing in different directions.

Lack of Commitment

Lack of commitment to educational reform follows in the wake of lack of agreed purpose and lack of direction. If there is a lack of agreed purpose and a lack of direction, it invariably results in a *lack of commitment* for education reform efforts. The characteristics of *lack of commitment* are

- lack of collaboration
- failed top-down control
- involvement of diverse groups
- failure to reach consensus among many organizations
- lack of vision and attainable goals
- no commitment possible without effective leadership and grass-roots empowerment

A lack of commitment to education reform and effective schools is a holdover from the recent past. *We need to understand the past if we are to work in the present and plan for the future.* The American educational landscape two decades ago created a disruptive atmosphere that created barriers to educational reform and effective schools. For example, decreased enrollments in our elementary and secondary schools, the property-tax revolt, divisive and often protracted strikes by teachers, civil rights, student due process and *equal protection* rights, busing, school mandates, racial violence and white flight, indictments that public schools were undemocratic (e.g., *Inequality* by Christopher Jencks), decline in high academic standards and academic achievement, and lack of confidence in the public schools,[9] clutched the focus of America. Educational reform and effective schools were not considered vital issues. A lack of agreed purpose and lack of direction led to a lack of commitment.

Other Educational Reform Failure Factors

If there is a lack of agreed purpose, a lack of direction, and a lack of commitment, "it is likely that a lack of effective leadership is a closely related reason for [educational] reform failure."[10] The research makes a strong case that *lack of effective leadership* is the foremost other reason for the failure of educational reform. Several other reasons were cited in the research on why educational reform failed.

- There was a lack of understanding of the complexity of the educational system and the conflicting organizations comprising it.
- Nearly all proposals to improve education ignored the interest groups that oppose reform.
- The educational system is so vast and complex that certain reforms could not be adopted.
- Schools, like other bureaucratic institutions, had developed strong protective mechanisms that preclude any meaningful kind of reform.
- The educational system itself gave resistance.

Some other reasons for educational reform failure that were referred to infrequently included lack of money, poorly qualified teachers, lack of student motivation, accommodation of new fads, loss of effective time in the classroom, conflicting values, annoyance with continued calls of crisis, cultural differences, and crisis of self-confidence of educators.[11] Most of these reasons were either directly or indirectly related to the three major reasons (see Figure 6.2) for educational reform failure.

An authentic example of agreed purpose, direction, and commitment occurred in 1957 when the Soviet Union launched Sputnik, an event which prompted the United States to immediate action. The National

```
┌─────────────────────────┐
│                         │
│        LACK  OF         │
│     AGREED  PURPOSE     │
│                         │
└─────────────────────────┘


┌─────────────────────────┐
│                         │
│        LACK  OF         │
│       DIRECTION         │
│                         │
└─────────────────────────┘


┌─────────────────────────┐
│                         │
│        LACK  OF         │
│      COMMITMENT         │
│                         │
└─────────────────────────┘
```

Figure 6.2 *Reasons for failure of educational reform.*

Defense Education Act was initiated and within a few years the United States not only orbited the earth, but it put a man on the moon.[12] Today, *Goals 2000: Educate America Act* (see Figure 6.3), passed by the United States Congress, has the potential to provide *world class* education standards for America. There is a definite purpose, direction, and commitment; however, the states must cooperate to make it happen.

The *Goals 2000: Educate America Act* is considered a mammoth reform bill that, for the first time, links local and state education improvement efforts with federal programs. It authorizes a $400 million federal program of grants to states and school districts that adopt reform plans. The directive is that plans for educational reform by the states "must contain high standards for curriculum content and student performance, as well as 'opportunity to learn' standards—which are essentially strategies for delivering adequate school services."[13]

INITIATING SCHOOL REFORM

History alone indicates that nothing less than the *best* education should be found in every community in the United States. To accomplish this,

By the year 2000 . . .

READINESS FOR SCHOOL

All children in America will start school ready to learn.

SCHOOL COMPLETION

The high school graduation rate will increase to at least 90 percent.

STUDENT ACHIEVEMENT AND CITIZENSHIP

All students will leave grades 4, 8, and 12 having demonstrated competency over challenging subjects including English, mathematics, science, foreign languages, civics and government, economics, arts, history, and geography, and every school in America will ensure that all students learn to use their minds well so they may be prepared for responsible citizenship, further learning, and productive employment in our nation's modern economy.

MATHEMATICS AND SCIENCE

U.S. students will be first in the world in mathematics and science achievement.

ADULT LITERACY AND LIFELONG LEARNING

Every adult American will be literate and will possess the knowledge and skills necessary to compete in the global economy and exercise the rights and responsibilities of citizenship.

SAFE, DISCIPLINED, AND ALCOHOL- AND DRUG-FREE SCHOOLS

Every school in the United States will be free of drugs, violence, and the unauthorized presence of firearms and alcohol and will offer a disciplined environment conducive to learning.

TEACHER EDUCATION AND PROFESSIONAL DEVELOPMENT

The nation's teaching force will have access to programs for the continued improvement of its professional skills and the opportunity to acquire the knowledge and skills needed to instruct and prepare all Americans for the next century.

PARENTAL AND FAMILY INVOLVEMENT

Every school will promote partnerships that will increase parental involvement and participation in promoting the social, emotional, and academic growth of children.

Figure 6.3 The national education goals.

a local school board must take the initial step by requesting from the school superintendent the development of a district plan for school improvement.[14] If this is done, an *agreed purpose* and *commitment* on the part of the local school board exists.

The school superintendent is now empowered by the board to create a district planning team that should consist of central office personnel, building-level administrators, teachers, community representatives, parents, and others. The superintendent must, to a large degree, assume the responsibility for charting educational *direction* for the people served in the community. The responsibility is even more profound today because

> . . . we have turned to the more difficult task, the education of those at the margins—those who have physical, mental, or emotional handicaps, those who have long been held at a distance by political or social means, and those who for a variety of reasons are less ready for what the schools have to offer and hence more difficult to teach.[15]

The superintendent and the district planning team have now overcome the three major barriers (lack of agreed purpose, lack of direction, and lack of commitment) to school reform (see Figure 6.4). The baton for

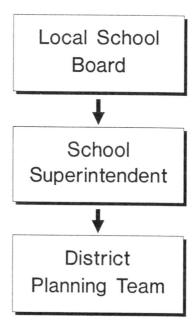

Figure 6.4 Initial steps for school improvement.

school improvement has been handed to the school superintendent. With the mandate by the school board, the chief executive officer of the board of education and educational leader in the community can demonstrate leadership and overcome another barrier to education reform, *lack of effective leadership*. This confidence in school administrators was echoed by President Clinton, when he was governor of Arkansas, by saying that "strong leaders create strong schools. Research and common sense suggest that [school] administrators can do a great deal to advance school reform." [16]

The superintendent and district planning team must ensure that a district plan for school improvement is based on the premise that *all* students can learn. The superintendent and district planning team are also responsible for the implementation, monitoring, and ongoing evaluation of the school improvement process as defined in the district plan (see Endnote 17 for the strategic planning source).

District Strategic Planning Process

To assist the superintendent and school district planning team in formulating the district development plan, the essential steps for initiating a strategic planning process are illustrated in Chapter 2, Figure 2.4. The process is dynamic because it involves all the stakeholders who will be given an opportunity to identify and create the necessary components for an effective school(s) in their community.

As the planning team proceeds in the process, it must constantly be cognizant of the characteristics that encompass effective schools. The extended research, from both empirical evidence and case studies of schools across the country, shows that schools that have been effective in teaching the *intended* curriculum to all the students had

- strong instructional leadership
- a clear and focused mission
- a climate of high expectations of success for all students
- a safe, orderly environment
- the opportunity to learn and enough time to spend on academic tasks
- frequent monitoring of student progress
- positive home-school relations [18]

Experience with different school districts throughout the nation has "taught us that school by school change will develop and be sustained *if* school change process occurs in the context of districtwide programs and procedures that help to sustain the focus." [19] By utilizing the strategic plan advocated in this book (see Chapter 2), changing school district programs and procedures will help to overcome the current barriers to educational reform. The educational program in every school district across the country is analogous to a house:

> This house was beautiful and well maintained, one of the nicest houses in the world. But over time, the owners allowed the house to deteriorate. First, a leak in the roof developed, allowing water to enter the attic, then trickle down to the second floor, and then to the main floor. Floors buckled, plaster fell from the walls, electric systems rusted, windows began to fall out. The owners, returning after a long absence, hastily repaired the windows, the plaster, and the electric motors—but they neglected to fix the roof. The owners were surprised and angry when, after all their efforts, the house continued to deteriorate. [20]

Like the house, appropriate planning by the school policymakers and school administrators will keep education in our communities from deteriorating and create a useful, productive future for the educational program in a community. Strategic planning will ascertain that the correct missions, goals, values, and needs are identified and used in selecting strategies and procedures.

ASSESSING EFFECTIVENESS OF SCHOOL POLICYMAKERS

In most journal articles and books on education, the focus is on what educators can or should do to create the right kind of learning environment for students in our schools. But there is much that cannot possibly be done without effective school policymakers, namely school boards. They have many duties and responsibilities; however, the three major functions, in rank order, for school board members are: (1) leadership and policymaking of a school or school district, (2) employment of school staff and supervision of the chief executive officer, the superintendent, and (3) representation of the constituency in their district.

Leadership and Policymaking

Constitutionally, all schools or school districts are required to have a board to conduct close and continual analyses of *organizational needs* and *direction.* How a board fulfills its management and policy responsibilities has "much, if not everything, to do with the quality of the schools." [21]

Employment and Supervision

The governing board of a school or school district must secure competent administrators and staff to uphold the standards of the organization. A governing board must free itself from the operational responsibility of a school or school district, but be accountable for the organization's success or failure. "The board's job is to govern, not manage." [22]

Representation of Constituency

School board members are elected or appointed officials that represent the people in their districts. "Representation must be for no individual or group bias, but it must be aimed at the basic long-term interests of the system [needs of students] and the community it serves." [23]

School board members are people who should respond positively to the following questions:

(1) Do you care about the success of learners after they leave your educational system and are citizens?

(2) Do you care about the quality – competence – of the completers and leavers when they leave your educational system?

(3) Do you care about the specific skills, knowledges, attitudes, and abilities of learners as they move from course to course, and level to level?

(4) Do you care about the efficiency of your educational programs, activities, and methods?

(5) Do you care about the quality and availability of your educational resources, including human, capital, financial, and learning?

(6) Do you care about the worth and value of your methods, means, and resources?

(7) Do you care about the extent to which you have reached your educational objectives? [24]

Caring alone, however, is not enough. For an organization to be effective, teamwork by school board members is essential. The "Test Your Togetherness Index," illustrated in Figure 6.5,[25] is a self-assessment questionnaire to help school board members evaluate their effectiveness.

All too often, school board members are referred to as *power people* because they (1) have their own agenda, (2) try to be political, (3) have strong beliefs, (4) are task oriented, and (5) are used to getting their own

The following questions can help you measure your school board's togetherness index. Answer each question using this five-point scale: 1 = strongly agree; 2 = tend to agree; 3 = neither agree nor disagree; 4 = tend to disagree; and 5 = strongly disagree.

1. My board effectively uses the strengths of each member. _____

2. Board members have confidence in one another's abilities. _____

3. Each member knows the strengths and weaknesses of other members. _____

4. Members give one another feedback about their contributions to the board's performance. _____

5. The board has team spirit. _____

6. Members work together effectively. _____

7. Members trust one another enough to share information, feedback, and personal thoughts honestly. _____

8. Members generally support one another. _____

9. Members believe they can trust their board colleagues when the chips are down. _____

TOTAL = _____

To determine your board's togetherness index, add the numbers you assigned to each statement and divide by 9. Generally, you are doing well if your score is 2.5 or less (the norm is 2.67).

INDEX = _____

Figure 6.5 *Test your togetherness index.*

way. Characteristics as such can only serve as barriers to providing the best educational opportunities for people in the school community. School board members working together can mold a winning team for education in their community.

Although the Tenth Amendment and state constitutions have not changed regarding who is responsible for education, American society has changed and will continue to change. Like society, education is an endless journey. Because of societal changes at the local, state, national, and global levels, collaboration and interdependence take on a new meaning for our school policymakers, educators, and citizens. As Nobel Prize winner, William Faulkner, indicated, ''Them that's going, get in the . . . wagon. Them that ain't, get out of the . . . way.''

REVIEW ACTIVITIES

(*1*) List the various reform movements with which your school has been involved. Discuss what contributing factors in terms of (a) lack of agreed purpose, (b) lack of direction, and (c) lack of commitment led to their ineffectiveness and demise. What other educational reform failure factors existed in your school during these failed reform movements? In other words, why did they fail?

(*2*) List the steps to effectively initiate school reform. Discuss how each step will empower reform.

(*3*) Refer to the seven characteristics that encompass effective schools. How do each of these empower school effectiveness? How can you develop the effective characteristics in your school?

(*4*) How can your school board members work together to mold a winning team for education in your community?

ENDNOTES

1 Vickery, T. R. 1990. "ODDM: A Workable Model for Total School Improvement," *Educational Leadership*, 47(7):67

2 United States Constitution, Amendment X.

3 South Dakota Constitution, Article VIII, Section 1, Uniform System of Free Public Schools.

4 Klein, M. F., ed. 1991. *The Politics of Curriculum Decision-Making*. Albany, NY: State University of New York Press, p. 1.

5 Wayson, W. 1988. *Up From Excellence: The Impact of the Excellence Movement on Schools.* Bloomington, IN: Phi Delta Kappan, p. 11.

6 Finn, C. E. and T. Rebarber, eds. 1992. *Education Reform in the 90s.* New York, NY: Macmillan, p. 157.

7 Heffner, F. D. 1993. "More Said Than Done: The History of Education Reform in the United States," Ed.D. diss., University of South Dakota.

8 ———. 1993. "More Said Than Done: The History of Education Reform in the United States," Ed.D. diss., University of South Dakota, p. 83.

9 Toch, T. 1991. *In the Name of Excellence.* New York, NY: Oxford University Press, pp. 4−9.

10 Heffner, F. D. 1993. "More Said Than Done: The History of Education Reform in the United States," Ed.D., diss., University of South Dakota, p. 88.

11 ———. 1993. "More Said Than Done: The History of Education Reform in the United States," Ed.D. diss., University of South Dakota, p. 75.

12 Boschee, F. 1989. "Has the United States Lost Its Competitive Edge or Commitment?" *NASSP Bulletin,* 73(517):79.

13 Walsh, M. 1994. "Main Events," *Education Vital Signs* (December edition):A4.

14 Cremin, L. A. 1976. *Public Education.* New York, NY: Basic Books, pp. 85−86.

15 Lezotte, L. W. and B. C. Jacoby. 1992. *Sustainable School Reform: The District Context for School Improvement.* Okemos, MI: Effective Schools Products, Ltd.

16 Amundson, K. 1988. "What Education Reports Say About Leadership," *Challenges for School Leaders.* Arlington, VA: American Association of School Administrators, p. 17.

17 For a complete school district or school strategic planning model, see Boschee, F. and M. A. Baron. 1993. *Outcome-Based Education: Developing Programs Through Strategic Planning.* Lancaster, PA: Technomic Publishing Co., Inc.

18 Lezotte, L. W. and B. C. Jacoby. 1992. *Sustainable School Reform: The District Context for School Improvement.* Okemas, MI: Effective Schools Products, LTD, p. 14.

19 Personal communication with Dr. Glen Robinson, President and Director of Research, Educational Research Service, Inc., Arlington, VA.

20 Hodgkinson, H. 1994. "Reform versus Reality," in *Effective School Board Governance.* W. K. Poston, Jr., ed. Bloomington, IN: Phi Delta Kappa Center for Evaluation, Development, and Research, p. 75.

21 Poston, W. K., Jr., ed. 1994. Introduction to *Effective School Board Governance.* Bloomington, IN: Center for Evaluation, Development, and Research.

22 ———. 1994. Introduction to *Effective School Board Governance.* Bloomington, IN: Phi Delta Kappa Center for Evaluation, Development, and Research.

23 ———. 1994. *Introduction to Effective School Board Governance.* Bloomington, IN: Phi Delta Kappa Center for Evaluation, Development, and Research.

24 Kaufman, R. 1994. Excerpts from "The Challenge of Total Quality Management in Education," in *Effective School Board Governance,* W. K. Poston, Jr., ed. Bloomington, IN: Phi Delta Kappa Center for Evaluation, Development, and Research, p. 38.

25 Banach, W. J. 1989. "Eleven Traits of Winning School Board Teams," *The American School Board Journal,* 176(10):23.

We have just completed a brief and lively journey through the perplexing terrain of public education. The authors have led us in engaging tours with stops such as strategic planning, vision, curriculum, school governance, and, above all, authentic student assessment. It has been an ambitious itinerary for them and for each of us readers.

I was particularly drawn to the manuscript by its title, *Authentic Assessment: The Key to Unlocking Student Success*. I have heard the term *authentic assessment* with increasing regularity in past months. I had a general sense of what it meant, but I wanted more. I have found it: I have found greater clarity and understanding in the preceding pages.

Authentic assessment seems an idea that has long been overdue. I'm glad it has come. I have always believed that student assessment is a kind of ''kingpin'' that holds together the precarious, aging erector set of public education. Touch it and you touch everything. Pull the pin—have the courage to challenge and the vision to replace conventional assessment—and the erector set collapses, and a new and more compelling structure that better serves youngsters and the adults who care so much about educating them begins to take form.

This is both the distinctive promise of authentic assessment and the danger. Authentic assessment is, indeed, a revolutionary concept.

Mark Baron and Floyd Boschee envision student assessment, not as numbers and letters and rank orderings and percentiles and bell-shaped curves, but, rather, as a powerful learning opportunity for young people and their teachers and parents. Authentic assessment offers a coherent new "kingpin," which demands that we diminish our pathological reliance upon timeworn "objective" measures of pupil performance. But, more, it reveals just how inadequate, even fraudulent, past evaluation practices have been in contributing to anyone's learning. And it is the promotion of learning, after all, that constitutes the reason for the existence of schools.

Authentic assessment is a new, and I believe far better, means of revealing what students know (whether the results can be readily translated into standardized measures or not). But what is truly revolutionary, and important, about authentic assessment is that the process makes visible to the student just what he or she has learned, gives a reason why they should learn it, and brings with it a *new* learning about themselves, about the skills needed to make visible what they know, and about the subject they have been learning. This is, indeed, a contribution to human learning.

There is a cost, as well as a gift, in making so visible what our youngsters are — or are not — learning in school. To be sure, implications exist for students who can no longer demonstrate learning by merely manipulating symbols. But the larger consequence — and more promising opportunity — is that the authentic revelation of what students know and don't know through exhibits, portfolios, and presentations focuses the limelight squarely upon educators who profess to be educating them. Authentic assessment is an evaluation not only of students as learners, but of educators as teachers. We can't lead where we will not go. Authentic assessment demands that teachers and principals, for instance, be themselves assessed like students — authentically. And the "exhibit" offered by teachers and principals is the learning of their students! A kingpin, indeed!

So, dear reader, join me in concluding this tidy little volume and in beginning to reconstruct our untidy, large educational system into one that young people and adults alike deserve — a school that is a community of learners and leaders.

ROLAND S. BARTH
Educational Consultant
and Founding Director,
The Principals' Center,
Harvard University

Mark A. Baron is assistant professor, Division of Educational Administration, School of Education, University of South Dakota, where he teaches graduate courses in educational administration, educational research, curriculum and instruction, strategic planning, community education, and outcome-based education. For almost twenty years, he was a teacher and principal in public and private schools located in the United States, Latin America, and West Africa. In addition to serving on the editorial board of *Research in the Schools,* he has presented numerous papers at national conferences, published widely in national journals, conducted numerous workshops for local school districts, and authored the book *Outcome-Based Education: Developing Programs Through Strategic Planning.*

Floyd Boschee is associate professor, Division of Educational Administration, School of Education, University of South Dakota, where he teaches and conducts research in educational leadership, supervision, curriculum, and outcome-based education. In eighteen years of public school service, he served as a teacher, coach, athletic director, and assistant superintendent for curriculum and instruction. He has also served as chairman of departments of education, published extensively in national journals, and authored the books, *Grouping = Growth, Effective Reading Programs: The Administrator's Role,* and *Outcome-Based Education: Developing Programs Through Strategic Planning.*